THE

ATHARVA-VEDA

Owing to the antiquity and rarity of this book, certain pages are regrettably absent, and readability is compromised due to the blurring of the original text. If you possess any insights regarding the availability of these missing sections, kindly inform us. Your assistance is crucial in ensuring the completion of this significant work for the benefit of future generations.

THE ATHARVA-VEDA

DESCRIBED ;

WITH

A classified Selection of Hymns, Explanatory Notes and Review

TRANSLATED

BY

RALPH T. H. GRIFFITH

GYAN

Published by

Gyan Publishing House
5, Ansari Road
Daryaganj, New Delhi-110002
Phone: 011-47034999, 9811692060
E-mail: books@gyanbooks.com

Distribution Network
gyanbooks.com
India, USA, Canada, UK, Australia

ISBN: 978-93-6280-268-2 (HB)
First Published, 1897

2nd Impression 2024

Printed at: Gyan Press, Delhi.

THE ATHARVA-VEDA

TRANSLATOR: RALPH T. H. GRIFFITH

THE

ATHARVA-VEDA

DESCRIBED;

WITH

A Classified Selection of Hymns, Explanatory Notes and Review.

FIRST EDITION, 3,000 COPIES.

THE CHRISTIAN LITERATURE SOCIETY FOR INDIA

LONDON AND MADRAS.

1897.

PREFATORY NOTE.

The following Selection of Hymns is taken from the Translation of the Atharva-Veda by Mr. R. T. H. Griffith, formerly Principal of Benares College. The Explanatory Notes are also abridged from the same source. Free permission to use the work was kindly given by the publishers, Messrs. E. J. Lazarus & Co., Benares, for which thanks are warmly returned.

The following works by Mr. Griffith are published by Messrs. Lazarus & Co.

HYMNS OF THE RIG-VEDA, translated with a Popular Commentary, 2 vols., 8vo. cloth bound, gilt lettered, Price Rs. 14.

HYMNS OF THE SAMA VEDA, as above. One volume, cloth bound, gilt lettered, Rs. 4. In stiff paper cover, Rs. 3¼.

HYMNS OF THE ATHARVA-VEDA, as above. Two vols. cloth, gilt lettered, Rs. 12. Stiff paper cover, Rs. 10½.

METRICAL TRANSLATION OF VALMIKI'S RAMAYANA, complete in one volume, 8vo. cloth, gilt lettered. Price Rs. 6.

Numerous other works in Sanskrit, Hindi, Urdu, and English have been published by Messrs. Lazarus & Co., Catalogue supplied on application.

CONTENTS.

Page

THE ATHARVA-VEDA.

INTRODUCTION.

Before noticing the Atharva-Veda, the fourth Veda, a brief account may be given of the three Vedas by which it is preceded.

Meaning of Term.—Veda is from the Sanskrit *vid*, 'know,' kindred with the Latin *vid*, and the English *to wit*. In its general sense it is sometimes applied by the Brahmans to the whole body of their most ancient sacred literature. More strictly, it denotes four collections of hymns, which are respectively known by the names of Rig-Veda, Yajur-Veda, Sama-Veda, and Atharva-Veda. They are supposed to contain *the* science, as teaching that knowledge which, of all others, is best worth acquiring.

"The general form of the Vedas is that of lyric poetry. They contain the songs in which the first ancestors of the Hindu people, at the very dawn of their existence as a separate nation, while they were still only on the threshold of the great country which they were afterwards to fill with their civilization, praised the gods, extolled heroic deeds, and sung of other matters which kindled their poetical fervour."*

The Vedas the highest Hindu Authorities.—The Hindu sacred books are divided into two great classes, called *Sruti* and *Smriti*. *Sruti*, which means hearing, denotes direct revelation; *Smriti*, recollection, includes the sacred books which are admitted to have been composed by human authors.

Professor Max Müller thus shows the estimation in which the Vedas are held:

"According to the orthodox views of Indian theologians, not a single line of the Veda was the work of human authors. The whole Veda is in some way or other the work of the Deity, and even those who received the revelation, or, as they express it, those who saw it, were not supposed to be ordinary mortals, but beings raised above the level of common humanity, and less liable therefore to error in the reception of revealed truth. .... The human element, called *paurusheyatva* in Sanskrit, is drawn out of every corner or hiding-place, and as the Veda is held to have existed in the mind of the Deity before the beginning of time, every allusion to historical events, of which there are not a few, is explained away with a zeal and ingenuity worthy of a better cause."

"The laws of Manu, according to the Brahmanic theology, are not revelation; they are not *Sruti*, but only *Smriti*. If these laws or any

---

* Whitney's *Oriental and Linguistic Studies*, Vol. I., p. 5.

other work of authority can be proved on any point to be at variance with a single passage of the Veda, their authority is at once overruled."*

The inspiration of the Veda, says Monier Williams, is regarded as so self-convincing, "as to require no proof, and to be entirely beyond the province of reason or argument."

According to Jaimini, the Vedas are *eternal,* because *sound is eternal!*

Dr. John Muir, in the Third Volume of his *Sanskrit Texts,* gives fourteen conflicting accounts of the origin of the Vedas, drawn from the authors themselves and from later Hindu writers. But as Max Müller remarks, "That one statement should be contradicted by another, seems never to have been felt as a serious difficulty"† by Hindus. Swami Vivekananda, at Chicago, "accepted all religions to be true"‡—theism and atheism, monotheism and polytheism.

Rig-Veda.—The name means the Veda of hymns of praise. *Rich,* which before the initial soft letter of Veda, is changed into *Rig,* is derived from a root which in Sanskrit means to celebrate. When standing by itself, *rich* becomes *rik.*

The hymns are called *Mantras* or *Suktas* (praises). The entire number form the *Sanhita* (or *Samhita*) collection. They are arranged in two methods. One divides them amongst eight *Kándas* (portions), or *Astakas* (eighths), each of which is again subdivided into eight *Adhyayas,* lectures. The other plan classes the *Suktas* under ten *Mandalas,* circles, subdivided into rather more than a hundred *Anuvakas,* or sub-sections. A further subdivision of the *Suktas* into *Vargas,* or paragraphs of about five stanzas each, is common to both classifications.§

As early as about 600 B.C. every verse, every word, every syllable had been carefully counted. The number of verses varies from 10,402 to 10,622; that of the *padas* or words, is 153,826; that of the syllables, 432,000.

The ten books form separate collections, each belonging to one of the ancient families of India.

The priests who specially recited the verses of the Rig-Veda were called *Hotris.*

An English translation of the Rig-Veda, based on the commentary of Sayana, was prepared by the late Professor Wilson. Part of it was published after his death. It is expensive, the price of the 6 volumes being £6-19s.

---

* *Chips from a German Workshop,* Vol. I.

† *Ancient Sanskrit Literature.* p. 321. Kapila was an exception. He says in his *Sánkhya Aphorisms,* Book I. "There is no acceptance of the inconsistent, else we come to the level of children, madmen and the like."

‡ *Report of Parliament of Religions,* p. 102.

§ Professor Wilson's Introduction, p. xiv.

The *Sacred Books of the East* contain two volumes of translations of *Vedic Hymns* by Max Müller and Oldenberg, prices 18*s*. 6*d*. and 14*s*. There is a complete translation of the whole book, with valuable explanatory notes, by Mr. R. T. H. Griffith, formerly Principal of Benares College; in two volumes, price Rs. 14, published by E. J. Lazarus and Co., Benares. With the kind permission of Mr. Griffith, some of the most important hymns from his translation are quoted in full in the work noted below.*

YAJUR-VEDA.—The name comes from *Yaj*, sacrifice. It contains the formulas and verses to be muttered by the priests and their assistants who had chiefly to prepare the sacrificial ground, to dress the altar, slay the victims, and pour out the libations.

The Black and White Yajus differ in their arrangement. In the former the sacrificial formulas are for the most part immediately followed by their explanation; in the latter they are entirely separated from one another.

A large portion of the materials of the Yajur-Veda is derived from the Rig-Veda, to about the half of which it is equal in both forms united. But it contains prose passages which are new.

As the manual of the priesthood, it became the great subject of study, and it has a great number of different Sakhas or Schools. The priests who used it were called *Adhvaryus*, offerers.

The text of both divisions has been printed either in India or in the West; but no English translation has yet been published.

SAMA-VEDA.—This is wholly metrical. It contains 1549 verses, only 78 of which have not been traced to the Rig-Veda. The verses have been selected and arranged for the purpose of being chanted at the sacrifices of which the intoxicating juice of the Soma plant was the chief ingredient. Many of the invocations are addressed to Soma, some to Agni, and some to Indra. There are special song books directing the manner in which they are to be intoned. The priests who recited the Sama-Veda were called *Udgatris*, chanters.

The text has been printed and there is an English translation by Mr. R. T. H. Griffith, published by Lazarus & Co., Benares. Price Rs. 4 cloth; Rs. 3¼ paper cover.

ATHARVA-VEDA.—This Veda is of later origin than the others. Manu speaks of only the Three Vedas. One-sixth of the work is in prose, and about one-sixth of the hymns is found in the Rig-Veda. A full account of it is given in the following pages.

So far as subject-matter is concerned, there may be said to be only two Vedas—The Rig and Atharva Vedas. The other two consist almost entirely of selections from the Rig-Veda, differently arranged for sacrificial purposes.

---

* *An Account of the Vedas, with Illustrative Extracts.* 8vo. 163 pp. 4½ As. Post-free, 6 As.

THE ATHARVA-VEDA.

Title.—Griffith gives the following explanation of the name:

"The Atharva-Veda is a comparatively late addition to the three ancient Vedas, the Rig, Yajus and Saman—the Vedas respectively of recited praise, sacrifice, and song or chanted hymn—which formed the foundation of the early religious belief and worship of the Hindus. Unlike these three Vedas, the Atharva-Veda derives the name by which it is generally known, not from the nature of its contents but from a person of indefinitely remote antiquity, named Atharvan, who is spoken of in the Rig-Veda as the first priest who 'rubbed Agni forth' or produced fire by attrition, who 'first by sacrifices made the paths' or established ways of communication between men and Gods, and overcame hostile demons by means of the miraculous powers which he had received from heaven. To the descendants of this Atharvan, associated with the Angirases and the Bhrigus, members of other ancient priestly families often mentioned in the Rig-Veda, the collected hymns—called also the Atharvángirasas and the Bhrigvangirasas, that is the Songs of the Atharvans and Angirases and the Songs of the Bhrigus and Angirases, and in the Gopatha-Bráhmana, the Atharvana-Veda and the Angirasa-Veda—were, it is said, originally revealed.—*Preface.*

Bloomfield, in the learned and elaborate Introduction to his translation, thus distinguishes between *Atharvan* and *Angiras*:

"The term Atharvan refers to the auspicious practices of the Veda, recognised as holy and 'conferring prosperity'; the term Angiras refers to the hostile sorcery practices of the Veda."*

It would seem, however, that this distinction was, at a later period, abandoned. Bloomfield says:

"In the end the name Atharvan and its derivatives prevail as designations of the practices and charms of the fourth Veda without reference to their strongly diversified character."†

Another name of the collection is *Brahma-Veda,* which is variously explained. Griffith considers it so called "as the Knowledge of Prayers (*brahmáni*), including benediction, imprecation, spells and charms—the Veda which teaches to appease the gods and secure their protecting favour, to bless friends, and to curse and destroy human and ghostly enemies, and all noxious creatures. It is the Veda of Prayers, Charms and Spells."‡

Age.—Griffith gives his own opinion and those of some eminent scholars on this point:

"I have called the Atharva-Veda a comparatively late addition to the three ancient Vedas, of which, it may be observed, one only, the Rig-Veda, is original and historical, the other two being merely liturgical compilations. The Atharva is like the Rik, in the main historical and

---

*Page xviii. Abridged. † *Ibid* p. xxiv. ‡ *Preface*, pp. I, II. Abridged.

original, but its contents cannot, as a whole, lay claim to equal antiquity."

Professor Whitney says:

'The greater portion of the hymns are plainly shown, both by their language and internal character, to be of much later date than the general contents of the other historic Veda, and even than its tenth book with which they stand nearly connected in import and origin. . . . This, however, would not imply that the main body of the Atharva hymns were not already in existence when the compilation of the Rik took place. Their character would be ground enough for their rejection and exclusion from the canon until other hands were found to undertake their separate gathering into an independent collection."

Professor Weber also observes:

"The origin of the Atharva Samhitá dates from the period when Brahmanism had become dominant. It is in other respects perfectly analogous to the Rik-Samhitá, and contains the store of song of this Brahmanical epoch. Many of these songs are to be found also in the last, that is the least ancient book of the Rik-Samhitá. In the latter they are the latest additions made at the time of its compilation. In the Atharvan they are the proper and natural utterance of the present. The spirit of the two collections is indeed widely different. In the Rik there breathes a lively natural feeling, a warm love for nature; while in the Atharvan there prevails, on the contrary, only an anxious dread of her evil spirits and their magical powers. In the Rik we find the people in a state of free activity and independence; in the Atharvan we see it bound in the fetters of the hierarchy and superstition. But the Atharva-Veda likewise contains pieces of great antiquity, which may perhaps have belonged more to the people proper, to its lower grades; whereas the songs of the Rik appear rather to have been the property of the higher families. It was not without a long struggle that the songs of the Atharvan were permitted to take their place as a fourth Veda. There is no mention made of them in the more ancient portions of the Bráhmanas of the Rik, Sáman, and Yajus."

Still, as Professor Max Müller says:

"The songs known under the name of the Atharvángirasas formed probably an additional part of the sacrifice from a very early time. They were chiefly intended to counteract the influence of any untoward event that might happen during the sacrifice. They also contained imprecations and blessings, and various formulas such as popular superstition would be sure to sanction at all times and in all countries. If once sanctioned, however, these magic verses would grow in importance, nay, the knowledge of the other Vedas would necessarily become useless without the power of remedying accidents, such as could hardly be avoided in so complicated a ceremonial as that of the Brahmans. As that power was believed to reside in the songs of the Atharvángirasas, a knowledge of these songs became necessarily an essential part of the theological knowledge of Ancient India."*

* *Preface*, pp. IV—VII.

Contrast between the Rig-Veda and the Atharva-Veda.—This is strongly set forth by Madame Ragozin, who attributes to the latter largely a non-Aryan origin :

"Nothing could well be imagined more different in contents and more opposite in spirit than these two *samhitás*. That of the Atharvan contains a comparatively small number of mantras from the Rig, and those only from the portions unanimously recognised as the latest, while the bulk of the collection along with some original hymns of the same kind and, in many cases, of great poetic beauty, consists chiefly of incantations, spells, exorcisms. We have here, as though in opposition to the bright, cheerful pantheon of beneficent deities, so trustingly and gratefully addressed by the Rishis of the Rig, a weird repulsive world of darkly scowling demons, inspiring abject fear, such as never sprang from Aryan fancy. We find ourselves in the midst of a goblin-worship, the exact counterpart of that with which we became familiar in Turanian Chaldea. Every evil thing in nature, from a drought to a fever or bad qualities of the human heart, is personified and made the object of terror-stricken propitiation, or of attempts at circumvention through witchcraft, or the instrument of harm to others through the same compelling force. Here and there, worship takes the form of conjuring, not prayer; its ministers are sorcerers, not priests. The conclusion almost forces itself on us, that this collection represents the religion of the native races, who, through a compromise dictated by a policy after a long period of struggle, ending in submission, obtained for it partial recognition from the conquering and every way superior race. It is easy to see how the latter, while condescending to incorporate the long abhorred ritual into their own canonical books, probably at first in some subordinate capacity, would, so to speak, sanctify or purify it, by supplementing it with some new hymns of their own, addressed to the same deities as those of the Rig and breathing the same spirit. If, as is more than probable, this is the history of the fourth Veda, the manner of its creation justifies the seemingly paradoxical assertion that it is at once the most modern of the four, and, in portions more ancient than even the oldest parts of the Rig-Veda. As a *samhitá*, it is a manifestly late production, since it bears evidence of having been in use in the valleys of the Gangá and the Yamuná; but the portions which embody an originally non-Aryan religion are evidently anterior to Aryan occupation."*

Double Aspect of the Atharva-Veda.—The following remarks on this point are abridged from Bloomfield :

"Many of the hymns and practices are benevolent and are in general well regarded, though even these do not altogether escape the blight of contempt. The class of charms designed to establish harmony in family and village life and reconciliation of enemies, are obviously auspicious in their nature. Even the sorceries of the Atharvan necessarily show a double face; they are useful to oneself, harmful to others. This conflict of emotions lasts throughout the history of the recorded Hindu

* *Vedic India*, pp. 117-119.

thought; the colour of the Atharvan remains changeable to the end, and is so described in the final orthodox and stereotyped view that it is used 'to appease, to bless, and to curse.' The fact, however, is that there must have arisen in the long run a strong wave of popular aversion against the Veda whose most salient teaching is sorcery. This appears from the discussions of the Hindus themselves as to the orthodoxy of that Veda; from the conscious efforts of the later Atharvan writings to vindicate its character and value; from the allegorical presentation of the Atharvan as 'a lean black man, sharp, irascible and amorous; and many occasional statements of the Vedic and classical texts." *

"Witchcraft blows hot and cold from the same mouth; according as it is turned towards the inimical forces, human and demoniac, or is turned by others against oneself, it is regarded as useful or noxious. Hymn II. 7, ensures protection against curses and hostile plots, but does not prevent the existence of fierce imprecations and curses issued forth subjectively for the ruin of another. It is a question throughout of my sorcery, or thy sorcery. †"

The Atharva-Veda in Hindu Literature.—Bloomfield, in his Introduction, devotes about thirty pages to this point, giving numerous references. Only a few books can be noticed.

Max Müller says in *Ancient Sanskrit Literature :*

"Because a knowledge of the songs of the Atharvángiras was most important to the Brahman or Purohita, these songs themselves, when once admitted to the rank of a Veda, were called the Veda of the Brahman, or the Brahma-Veda."

The Rev. Dr. K. S. Macdonald, after quoting the above, adds :

"In the Gopatha Bráhmana they are repeatedly represented as the proper Veda for the Brahman. Thus we read (iii. i.) : 'Let a man elect a Hotri, who knows the Rich, an Adhvaryu who knows the Yajush, an Udgatri who knows the Sáman, a Brahman who knows the Atharvángiras.' "‡

Manu thus advises the Brahman :

"Let him use without hesitation the sacred texts revealed by Atharvan and by Angiras; speech, indeed, is the weapon of the Brahman, with it he may slay his enemies." XI. 33.

In the Mahábhárata its importance as a Veda, and its canonicity, are finally and completely established ; its practices are familiarly known, and, in general, not subjected to any peculiar criticism.'§

"The Purãnas always speak of the fourfold Veda."||

Versification.—In the Preface to his translation, Griffith says :

"The prevailing metres of the original hymns are Gáyatrí, Anushtup, Pankti, Trishtup, and Jagatí, consisting the first three of three, four, and five octosyllabic Pádas or divisions, and the last two of four hendecasyllabic and dodecasyllabic Pádas respectively. In translating

* *Introduction*, p. xxix. † *Ibid*, p. xxxix.

‡ *Indian Evangelical Review*, July, 1897 p. 55.

§ *Bloomfield's Introduction*, p. li. || *Ibid*, p. lv.

the first set I have employed corresponding numbers of the common octosyllabic or dimeter iambic line, and in the second of the ordinary hypercatalectic blank verse line and the Alexandrine." *Preface*, p. XVII.

A fuller account of the metres employed in the Vedas will be found in the Introduction to the *Account of the Vedas.*

"Parts of the Atharva-Veda, for instance Book XV. and the greater portion of XVI., are entirely in prose, and hymns, verses, and parts of verses in prose are found in other Books also. "It is not possible," as Professor Whitney observes, 'to draw everywhere a sharp line between metrical and non-metrical matter; prose and loose verse slide into one another sometimes in a perplexing manner, or are mixed up in the same stanza.' "

Divisions.—Griffith gives the following general view:

"The Atharva-Veda Sanhitá or Collection is divided into twenty *Kándas*, Books or Sections, containing some 760 hymns and about 6,000 verses. In Books I.—VII. the hymns or pieces are arranged according to the number of their verses, without any reference to their subjects or the nature of their contents. The hymns of Book I. contain on an average four verses each; those of Book II. five; those of III. six; those of IV. seven; those of V. from eight to eighteen; those of VI. three; those of VII. many single verses and upwards to eleven. Books VIII.—XX contain longer pieces, some of which extend to 50, 60, 70, and even 80 verses. In Books I.—XIII. the contents are of the most heterogeneous description. with no attempt at any kind of systematic arrangement of subjects. They consist principally of prayers, formulas and charms for protection against evil spirits of all sorts and kinds, against sorcerers and sorceresses, diseases, snakes, and other noxious creatures, of benedictions and inprecations, invocations of magical herbs, prayers for children and long life, for general and special protection and prosperity, success in love, trade and gambling, together with formulas to be employed in all kinds of domestic occurrences. In Books XIV.—XVIII. the subjects are systematically arranged; XIV. treating of marriage ceremonies; XV. of the glorification of the Vrátya or religious wandering mendicant; XVI. and XVII. of certain conjurations; XVIII. of funeral rites and the offering of obsequial cakes to the Manes or spirits of departed ancestors. Book XIX. contains a somewhat miscellaneous collection of supplementary hymns. Book XX. consists—with the exception of what is called the Kuntápa Section, comprising hymns 127—136—of pieces addressed to Indra and taken entirely from the Rig-Veda. These two Books, which are not noticed in the Atharva-Veda Prátísákhya—a grammatical treatise on the phonetic changes of words in the text—are manifestly a later addition to the collection. Many of the Atharva hymns reappear in the Rig-Veda, about one-seventh of the collection, sometimes unchanged and sometimes with important variations, being found in the older compilation. Interspersed in several of the Books are pieces of varying length, consisting of curious cosmological and mystico-theological speculations which are not without interest as containing the germs of religious and philosophical doctrines

* Preface, pp. XVII., XVIII.

afterwards fully developed in the Bráhmanas and Upanishads." *Preface*, pp. VII, VIII.

General Character.—Griffith gives the following summary :—

"In this strange collection of heterogenous material there is much that is obscure, much that is unintelligible, much that is intolerably tedious, and not a little that is offensive and disgusting to European taste. Yet the spiritual portions of the work have sometimes a strange beauty and grandeur of their own which attracts and fascinates the orthodox Hindu, while the occasional glimpses of light which it throws upon the daily life, the toils and pleasures, the hopes and fears, the joys and sorrows of the average man invests it, I think, for the European reader with greater and more human interest than is possessed by the more ancient Veda." *Preface*, pp. VIII, IX.

Griffith next skilfully groups the hymns together so as to give a vivid picture of life in all its aspects in the times of the Atharva-Veda. This is quoted under another head.

Text.—Griffith says:

"The text of the Atharva-Veda, with 'some amendments of the numerous and obvious false readings of the manuscripts, and some attempts to bring sense out of the utter nonsense which constitutes part of the last two books,' was published at Berlin, in 1856, by Professors Rudolf von Roth and W. D. Whitney." *Preface*, p. XIII.

English Translations.—Some entire hymns and many fragments are given in Muir's *Original Sanskrit Texts.* The first complete English translation published is by Mr. R. T. H. Griffith, noticed in the Preface, from which the following extracts are taken. There are also numerous useful notes, forming a commentary on the hymns. In two volumes, price Rs. 12 cloth, Rs. 10½ paper covers.

The *Hymns of the Atharva-Veda,* translated by Professor Maurice Bloomfield, John Hopkins University, United States, has recently been added to the *Sacred Books of the East.* The author says:

"The present volume of translations comprises about one-third of the entire material of the Atharva-Veda. But it represents the contents and spirit of the fourth Veda in a far greater measure than is indicated by this numerical statement." p. lxxi.

Passages that occur in the Rig-Veda, books in prose, and hymns of less interest, have been omitted.

"Of the rest of the Atharvan, (Books I-XIII) there is presented here about one-half, naturally that half which seemed to the translator the most interesting and characteristic." p. lxxii.

The hymns in Bloomfield's translation are classified according to subject-matter. Griffith gives the whole in the original order.

2

Each plan has its advantages. With a limited number of hymns perhaps the former is preferable.

Bloomfield's translation is followed by a learned commentary. It is published by the Clarendon Press, Price 21*s*.

SUMMARY OF THE BOOKS.

A short general view of the Books is given in the Introduction. The following account enters more into detail.

Book I.

This Book contains 35 Hymns, each averaging 4 verses. The subjects are very miscellaneous, and there is no arrangement.

The first hymn, quoted below, introductory to the whole Book, is a prayer addressed to Váchaspati for divine help, favour, and illumination. Váchaspati, Lord of Speech, is the God or Genius of human life which lasts as long as the power of speech remains in the body. Vasoshpati, Lord of Treasure, that is of wealth and food, is not mentioned elsewhere in the Veda. (Griffith.)

1. Now may Váchaspati assign to me the strength and powers of Those
   Who, wearing every shape and form, the triple seven, are wandering round.
2. Come thou again, Váchaspati, come with divine intelligence.
   Vasoshpati, repose thou here. In me be Knowledge, yea, in me.
3. Here, even here, spread sheltering arms like the two bow-ends strained with cord.
   This let Váchaspati confirm. In me be knowledge, yea, in me.
4. Váchaspati hath been invoked: may he invite us in reply.
   May we adhere to Sacred Lore. Never may I be reft thereof.

NOTES.—*Those*: the gods in general, or the Maruts. *The triple seven*: an indefinite number.

Book II.

This Book contains 36 Hymns of a miscellaneous character, averaging 5 verses in length.

Book III.

This Book contains 31 Hymns of the same character as the preceding, but averaging 6 verses each. Hymn 16 is the morning prayer of the great Rishi, Vasishtha, taken, with slight variation, from Rig-Veda VII. 41. The chief petitions are, "give us wealth," "may we be rich in men and heroes."

Book IV.

In this Book 40 Hymns, averaging 7 verses, are included. Hymn 2, an address to the Unknown God, is from Rig-Veda X. 121. There are other Hymns from the same Veda.

Book V.

This Book contains 31 Hymns, averaging 12 verses. One is a curious dialogue between Atharva and Varuna about the possession of a wonderful cow. Another is about the abduction of a Brahman's wife. Two Hymns are on the wickedness and ruinous consequences of oppressing Brahmans. Two are addressed to the War Drum to secure success in battle.

Book VI.

Of the 142 Hymns in this Book most contain only 3 verses. They consist of prayers and charms.

Book VII.

This Book contains 118 Hymns, nearly one-half of which consist of only a single verse. The contents are like the foregoing.

Book VIII.

This Book contains only 10 Hymns, but they average 26 verses in length. They consist chiefly of imprecations or charms for the restoration of health. Hymn 4, against evil spirits, is taken from Rig-Veda VII. 104.

Book IX.

This Book contains 10 Hymns; one of which is entirely in prose, while a second has only two stanzas in verse out of 62. The longest is "a glorification of the hospitable reception of guests, regarded as identical with sacrifice offered to the gods." Hymns 9 and 10, consisting of enigmatical questions, are taken, with variations, from Rig-Veda I. 164.

Book X.

This Book contains 10 Hymns, averaging 35 verses. One is a glorification of the Supreme Deity, under the name of Skambha, considered the Pillar or Support of all existence. Another is in praise of the Sacred Cow.

Book XI.

This Book contains 10 Hymns, averaging 31 verses, Hymn 3, which is all in prose except 4 lines, is in praise of the offering of rice boiled in milk. Hymn 8 treats of the origin of several gods and the creation of man. The last two Hymns are incantations for the destruction of enemies.

Book XII.

This Book contains only 5 Hymns, but they average 60 verses. The second is a funeral hymn, taken partly from Rig-Veda X. 18. Hymns 4 & 5, the latter partly in prose, show the sin and danger of robbing a Brahman of his cow.

Book XIII.

This Book contains 4 Hymns, averaging 47 verses. "It is almost entirely devoted to the glorification of Rohita, the Red, a form of Fire and of the Sun, but distinguished from both these deities."

Book XIV.

This Book contains only 2 Hymns, including 139 verses. It treats of nuptial ceremonies and formulas. The greater part of Hymn 1 is taken, with many changes, from Rig-Veda X. 85; Hymn 2 is also partly taken from the same hymn.

Book XV.

This Book contains 18 Hymns, averaging about 10 stanzas. They are all in prose and very obscure. The aim seems to be the glorification of the Vrátya, or wandering Nonconformist.

Book XVI.

This Book contains 9 Hymns, averaging 10 verses. Some of them are entirely in prose; others partly in prose and partly in poetry. "The Book consists almost entirely of charms and conjurations for various purposes."

Book XVII.

This Book contain only one Hymn, including 30 verses. It is a prayer to Indra, identified with Vishnu and the Sun, for the love of gods, men, and beasts, general protection and prosperity, with all earthly and heavenly blessings."

Book XVIII.

This Book contains 4 Hymns, averaging 70 verses. "The subjects are funeral rites and sacrificial offerings to the Fathers, the manes or spirits of the dead." The Hymns are composed wholly or in part from verses in the Rig-Veda. The first Hymn begins with a dialogue between Yama and Yami.

Book XIX.

This Book contains 72 Hymns, averaging about 8 verses. Both it and the following are later additions to the original collection. The MSS. contain numerous misreadings which in some parts make utter nonsense. The Hymns are chiefly prayers and charms for protection and prosperity. Hymn 6, on the mystical sacrifice of Purusha, is taken, with variations, from Rig-Veda X. 90. Hymn 13, a prayer for victory in battle, is taken from Rig-Veda X. 103. Some Hymns are non-metrical. Hymn 21 gives in a single line the names of the chief Vedic Metres:

Gáyatrí, Ushnih, Anushtup, Brihatí, Trishtup, Jagatí.

Hymn 23, all in prose except one verse, is an address of homage to various portions of the Atharva-Veda, classed according to the number of verses which their hymns contain.

1 Hail to the four verse strophes of the Atharvanas! 2 Hail to the five versed! 3 Hail to the six-versed, &c.

30 Collected manly powers are topped by Brahma.
Brahma at first spread out the loftiest heaven.
Brahmá was born first of all things existing.
Who then is fit to be this Brahmá's rival?

Book XX.

This Book contains 143 Hymns of various lengths, but averaging about 8 verses. With the exception of the Kuntápa section (127-136) the Hymns are addressed almost exclusively to Indra, and generally taken directly from hymns and portions of hymns of the Rig-Veda.

Kuntápa is said to be the name of 20 organs or glands, supposed to be situated in the belly. The section is a strange collection of incantations riddles, &c., without any religious character. With some of them the gods bewildered the Asuras by their recitation, and so defeated them.

CLASSIFIED SELECTION OF HYMNS.

Belief in Witchcraft and the power of Charms forms distinguishing features of the Atharva-Veda. Bloomfield says in his Introduction:

"Sorcery and house practices there were in India at all times (p. xxx). Witchcraft is blended with every sphere of religious thought and activity (p. xxxix). Even Witchcraft is part of the religion; it has penetrated and has become intimately blended with the holiest Vedic rites." (xlv.)

Among the aboriginal tribes of India all diseases in men or animals are attributed to one of two causes—the anger of some evil spirit who has to be appeased or to the spell of some witch or sorcerer, who should be destroyed or driven out of the land. In the latter case, a witchfinder is employed to divine who has cast the spell, and various modes of divination are resorted to. In former times the person denounced and all his family were put to death in the belief that witches breed witches. We have changed all that. "The witch now," says Sir Alfred Lyall, "lives under laws which, instead of condemning him, interfere actively to protect him from molestation, and are much more prone to hang witch-finders than witches. . . . It is probable that in no other time or country is witchcraft ever been so comfortably practised as it is now in India under British rule."* He says that "the belief in witchcraft still pervades all classes (in India), from highest to lowest (though of course the pressure of the superstition is far lighter upon the uppermost layers of society)."†

In the charms plants are frequently employed. They do not exert a medicinal influence; but, from illusory analogies, are supposed to have peculiar powers. A creeping plant which binds itself to a tree is supposed to be able to cure broken bones; another which has strong deep roots must be able to make the hair grow.

Charms are of two kinds—to preserve from harm or to cause harm. Illustrative examples will now be given.

1. CHARMS TO CURE DISEASE.

The householder and his family are exposed to malarial fevers and other diseases to which flesh is heir. A large number of hymns have reference to their cure. Even baldness has three hymns. For ready reference, the principal charms are arranged alphabetically.

Bloodletting.—Book I. 17.

1 Those maidens there, the veins who run their course in robes of ruddy hue,
Must now stand quiet, reft of power, like sisters who are brotherless.

2 Stay still, thou upper vein, stay still, thou lower, stay, thou midmost one.
The smallest one of all stands still : let the great vessel e'en be still.

4 A mighty rampart‡ built of sand hath circled and encompassed you :
Be still, and quietly take rest.

Broken Bone.—IV. 12. An address to the plant Arundhati, a climbing plant, to bind the injured limb as it binds the tree round which it grows :

1 Thou art the healer, making whole, the healer of the broken bone :
Make thou this whole, Arundhati !

2 Whatever bone of thine within thy body hath been wrenched or cracked,
May Dhatar§ set it properly, and join together limb by limb.

* *Asiatic Studies*, p. 96. † *Ibid.*, p. 75.

‡ Probably a bandage filled with wet sand to compress and cool the vein.

§ The god who ordains, fixes, and preserves.

5 Join thou together hair with hair, join thou together skin with skin.
Let blood and bone grow strong in thee. Unite the broken part, O Plant.

Consumption.—VI. 14. There are frequent references to this disease, which is still prevalent. It is fostered among women by their being often shut up in close rooms without a sufficient supply of pure air. Hymn II. 33 is enlarged with variations from Rig-Veda X. 163. The hymn quoted below is a charm addressed to some medicinal plant.

1 Remove thou all Decline that lurks within the members and the joints.
The firmly-settled heart-disease that racks the bones and rends the limbs.
2 From the consumptive man I pluck Decline as 'twere a creeping thing.
I cut the bond that fetters him, even as a root of cucumber.
3 Begone, Consumption, hence away, like a young foal that runs at speed.
Then, not pernicious to our men, flee, yearly visitant like grass!

Cough.—VI. 105.

1 Rapidly as the fancy flies forth with conceptions of the mind,
So following the fancy's flight, O Cough, flee rapidly away.
2 Rapidly as an arrow flies away with keenly-sharpened point,
So swiftly flee away, O Cough, over the region of the earth!
3 Rapidly as the beams of light, the rays of Súrya, fly away,
So, Cough! fly rapidly away over the current of the sea!

Dysentery.—I. 2. An arrow and munja grass are employed.

1 We know the father of the shaft, Parjanya, liberal nourisher,
Know well his mother Prithivi, Earth with her manifold designs.
2. Do thou, O Bowstring, bend thyself around us; make my body stone (=strong).
Firm in thy strength drive far away malignities and hateful things.
3 When, closely clinging round the wood (the bow) the bowstring sings triumph to the swift and whizzing arrow, Indra, ward off from us the shaft, the missile:
4 As in its flight the arrow's point hangs between earth and firmament,
So stand this Munja grass between ailment and dysenteric ill!

The succeeding hymns treat of reverse diseases—constipation and suppression of urine. As an arrow from a bow flies through the air, so the channels are to flow.

Fever, Charms against.—Susruta calls fever the king of diseases. It causes more deaths in India than all other diseases taken together. There are several charms for its cure. In Hymn I. 25, quoted below, it is said to be more frequent at the beginning of the rains when Agni descends, in the form of lightning, from the water clouds. Bilious fever causes the yellow colour. Other forms of the disease are mentioned. Fever is addressed as a god, the son of King Varuna, sent to punish sin. Yielding to prayer, he is asked to depart.

1 When Agni blazed when he had pierced the Waters,
whereat the Law observers paid him homage,
There, men assever, was the loftiest birthplace:
O Fever, yielding to our prayer avoid us.

2 If thou be fiery glow, or inflammation, or if thy birthplace call for chips of fuel,
Rack is thy name, God of the sickly yellow!
O Fever, yielding to our prayer avoid us.

3 Be thou distress, or agonizing torment, be thou the son King Varuna hath begotten,
Rack is thy name, God of the sickly yellow!
O Fever yielding to our prayer avoid us,

4 I offer homage to the chilly Fever, to his fierce burning glow I offer homage.
Be adoration paid to Fever coming each other day, the third, or two days running.

Hymn 116 Book VII. contains another charm against fever. A frog, which has two strings of different colours tied round it, is supposed to relieve the patient of his disease.

1 Homage to him the burning one, shaker, exciter, violent!
Homage to him the cold who acts according to his ancient will!

2 May he, the lawless one, who comes alternate or two following days, pass over and possess the frog.

Hair, Charm to promote the growth.—There are three charms for this object. In Hymn 136, Book VI. quoted below, a plant with deep roots, and therefore supposed to strengthen the hair, is employed.

1 Born from the bosom of wide Earth the goddess, godlike Plant, art thou:
So we, Nitatní! dig thee up to strengthen and fix fast the hair.

2 Make the old firm, make new hair spring, lengthen what has already grown.

3 Thy hair where it is falling off, and with the roots is torn away,
I wet and sprinkle with the Plant, the remedy for all disease.

Headache.—Hymn 8 Book IX. is for the cure of various diseases and pains more or less connected or supposed to be connected with consumption. The first two stanzas, quoted below, treat of Headache, Earache, &c.

1 Each pain and ache that racks the head, earache, and erysipelas,
All malady that wrings thy brow we charm away with this our spell.
2 From both thine ears, from parts thereof, thine earache, and the throbbing pain,
All malady that wrings thy brow we charm away with this our spell.

Insanity.—In Hymn 111, Book VI. a man is described as insane either as a punishment for sin or caused by a demon. Agni, the Apsarasas, goddesses of gambling, "Maddeners of the mind," Indra and Bhoja, are asked to let him go.

1 Unbind and loose for me this man, O Agni, who bound and well restrained is chattering folly.
Afterward he will offer thee thy portion when he hath been delivered from his madness.
2 Let Agni gently soothe thy mind when fierce excitement troubles it.
Well-skilled I make a medicine that thou no longer mayst be mad.
3 Insane through sin against the gods, or maddened by a demon's power—
Well-skilled I make a medicine to free thee from insanity.
4 May the Apsarasas release, Indra and Bhaga let thee go.
May all the gods deliver thee that thou no longer mayst be mad.

Jaundice.—Hymn 22, Book I., of which two verses are quoted below, is partly taken from Rig-Veda I. 50. The Romans supposed that the disease was cured by looking at a starling, which died instead of the patient.

1 As the Sun rises let thy sore disease and yellowness depart.
We compass and surround thee with the colour of a ruddy ox.
4 To parrots and to starlings we transfer thy sickly yellowness:
Now in the yellow-coloured birds we lay this yellowness of thine.

Leprosy.—Susruta describes seven forms of this terrible disease, and eleven slighter forms. Plants were employed in the charms for its cure. There are other hymns on the same subject.

I. 23.

1 O Plant, thou sprangest up at night, dusky, dark-coloured, black in hue!
So, Rajaní, re-colour thou these ashy spots, this leprosy.
2 Expel the leprosy, remove from him the spots and ashy hue:
Let thine own colour come to thee; drive far away the specks of white.
3 Dark is the place of thy repose, dark is the place thou dwellest in;
Dusky and dark, O Plant, art thou; remove from him each speck and spot.

4 I with my spell have chased away the pallid sign of leprosy
Caused by infection, on the skin, sprung from the body, from the bones.

Nightmare and Evil Dreams.—There are some references to these which are asked to be transferred to enemies. In some parts of India nightmare is supposed to be caused by a demon seated on the breast, attempting to strangle the person affected.

VII. 100.

1 I turn away from evil dream, from dream of sin, from indigence, I make the prayer mine inmost friend. Hence! torturing dreamy phantasies!

VI. 46.

2 We know thy birth, O Sleep, thou art son of the sisters of the Gods! the minister of Yama thou, thou art Antaka (the Finisher), thou art Death.
So well we know thee who thou art. Sleep, guard us from the evil dream.
3 As men discharge a debt, as they pay up an eighth and half-an-eighth,
So the whole evil dream do we pay and assign unto our foe.

Poison, Against.—There are several hymns on this subject—against poisoned arrows, to render poisonous plants innocuous, &c. In Hymn 90, Book VI., quoted below, Rudra is addressed as the terrible god whose shafts bring diseases and death on men and cattle.

1 The shaft that Rudra hath shot forth against thy members and thy heart,
Here do we draw from thee to-day, and turn it hence to every side.
2 From all the hundred vessels spread throughout the members of thy frame,
From all those vessels and canals we call the poisonous matter forth.
3 Worship to thee, the archer, and O Rudra, to thy levelled shaft!
Yea, worship to thine arrow when it left the bow, and when it fell.

Snakes, Scorpions, Musquitoes, &c.—There are several references to snakes. Hymn 56, Book VI. begins:

Let not the serpent slay us, O Gods, with our children and our folk.

Hymn 56, Book VII. is a charm against bites and stings of various kinds, for which purpose a plant is employed. Brahmanaspati is addressed as the god of charms and prayer.

1 Whether it came from viper, from black snake or snake with transverse stripes,
Or Kankaparvan's bite, this herb hath made the poison powerless.

2 Honey-born, honey-dropping, rich in honey, honey-sweet, this herb
Is medicine that heals the wound and kills the gnat that bites and stings.
3 Whatever bit or sucked thy blood, we summon thence away from thee.
The ineffectual poison of the little sharply-stinging gnat.
4 Thou here who crookest wicked jaws, thou tortuous, jointless, limbless thing,
These jaws thou, Brahmanaspati! shalt bend together like a reed.
5 This scorpion here that creeps along, low on the ground and powerless—
I have removed his poison and then utterly demolished him.
6 No strength in thy two arms hast thou, nor in thy head, nor in thy waist:
Then what is that small thing thou so viciously bearest in thy tail?
7 The emmets make a meal of thee and peahens tear and mangle thee:
All ye are crying out, In sooth the scorpion's poison hath no strength.
8 Thou creature who inflictest wounds both with thy mouth and with thy tail,
No poison in thy mouth hast thou: what at thy tail's root will there be?

Tigers, Wolves, Thieves, etc.—IV. 3. The tiger, frequently mentioned in the Atharva-Veda, seems to have been unknown to the writers of the Rig-Veda. The 'tiger-crushing charm' is supposed to have been a poisonous plant, deriving its growth from Soma, king of plants, and its poison from Indra. Its origin is ascribed to the ancient fire-priest, Atharvan:

1 Three have gone hence and passed away, the man, the tiger, and the wolf.
3 We crush and rend to pieces both thine eyes, O Tiger, and thy jaws, and all thy twenty claws we break.
5 The thief who cometh near to-day departeth bruised and crushed to bits.
By nearest way let him be gone. Let Indra slay him with his bolt.
7 Indra's and Soma's child, thou art Atharvan's tiger-crushing charm.

Worms.—II. 31. The charm is against worms of various kinds, those found in plants, in water, in human beings, and in cattle. Two verses are quoted, "Indra's mighty millstone" denotes his great power. The next hymn, 32, is against worms in cows.

1 With Indra's mighty millstone, that which crushes worms of every sort,
I bray and bruise the worms to bits like vetches on the grinding stone.

5 Worms that are found on mountains, in the forests, that live in plants, in cattle, in the waters,
Those that have made their way within our bodies,—these I destroy, the worms' whole generation.

Wounds. VI. 57.—Rudra is the healer as well as the inflicter of wounds and diseases.

1 This is a medicine indeed, Rudra's own medicine is this,
Wherewith he warns the arrow off, one-shafted, with a hundred tips.
2 Besprinkle it with anodyne, bedew it with relieving balm:
Strong, soothing is the medicine: bless us therewith that we may live.
3 Let it be health and joy to us. Let nothing vex or injure us.
Down with the wound! Let all to us be balm, the whole be medicine.

Charm to recover from the Point of Death or even to recall the departed Spirit.—There are three hymns thus entitled. Hymn 1, Book VIII. is partly quoted below:

Mátarisvan is a name of Váyu or Wind.

1 Homage to Death the Ender! May thy breathings, inward and outward, still remain within thee.
Here stay this man united with his spirit in the Sun's realm, the world of life eternal!
2 Bhaga hath lifted up this man, and Soma with his filaments.
Indra and Agni, and the gods the Maruts, raised him up to health.
3 Here is thy spirit, here thy breath, here is thy life, here is thy soul;
By a celestial utterance we raise thee from Destruction's bonds.
4 Up from this place, O man, rise! sink not downward, casting away the bonds of Death that hold thee.
Be not thou parted from this world, from sight of Agni and the Sun.
5 Purely for thee breathe Wind and Mátarisvan, and let the Waters rain on thee their nectar.
The Sun shall shine with healing on thy body; Death shall have mercy on thee; do not leave us!
6 Upward must be thy way, O man, not downward: with life and mental vigour I endow thee.
Ascend this car eternal, lightly rolling; then full of years shalt thou address the meeting.
7 Let not thy soul go thither, nor be lost to us; slight not the living, go not where the Fathers are.
Let all the gods retain thee here in safety.
8 Yearn not for the departed ones, for those who lead men far away.
Rise up from darkness into light; come, both thy hands we clasp in ours.

9 Let not the black dog and the brindled seize thee, two warders of the way sent forth by Yama.
Come hither; do not hesitate: with mind averted stay not there.
10 Forbear to tread this path, for it is awful; that path I speak of which thou hast not travelled.
Enter it not, O man; this way is darkness; forward is danger, hitherward is safety.

. . . . .

. . . . . .

18 Here let this man, O Gods, remain! let him not go to yonder world.
We rescue him from Mrityu with a charm that hath a thousand powers.
19 I have delivered thee from Death. Strength-givers smelt and fashion thee!
Let not she-fiends with wild loose locks, or fearful howlers yell at thee.
20 I have attained and captured thee! thou hast returned restored to youth,
Perfect in body: so have I found all thy sight and all thy life.
21 Life hath breathed on thee; light hath come: darkness hath past away from thee.
Far from thee we have buried Death, buried Destruction and Decline.

Prayers or Charms for Long Life.—In the times of the Atharva-Veda, the later gloomy views of life had not arisen. Long life is frequently desired. In the original home of the Aryans, "the complete term of life" was computed at a 'hundred *winters*. As they moved farther south, *autumns* were substituted, and lastly *rainy seasons* (*varsháni.*)

Hymn 69, Book XIX., quoted below, is in prose. The gods are supposed to be dependent on the sacrifices of men, as the worshipper is dependent on the gods.

1. Ye are alive. I fain would live. I fain would live my complete term of life. 2. Ye live dependent. I fain would live dependent. I fain would live my complete term of life. 3. Ye remain alive. I fain would remain alive. I fain would live my complete term of life. 4. Ye are life-givers. I fain would live. I fain would live my complete term of life.

CHARMS WITH AMULETS.

An Amulet is something worn as a remedy or preservative against evils or mischief, such as diseases or witchcraft. Amulets have been used from very ancient times, and are still worn in many parts of the world. In some parts of Africa negroes are almost covered with them.

Some object was employed supposed to possess magical powers. Plants were often chosen. Some of them have already been mentioned as remedies for disease. *Arundhati,* a medicinal climbing plant, was frequently used. The *Asvattha,* the pipal, or sacred fig-tree, was still more popular. In Hymn 4, Book V. the gods are said to sit under its shade in the third heaven. The *Kusa* or *Darbha* grass was supposed to possess sanctifying qualities. *Munja grass* was employed as a spell to cure dysentery. The *Jangida,* a plant not yet identified, is frequently mentioned as a charm against demons, and a specific for various diseases. The wood of the *Udumbara Fig-tree* was sometimes used. The wood of the *Tilaka* tree was supposed to ward off witchcraft. Several other plants, not yet identified, were also used as amulets.

The *horn* of the roebuck was employed to drive away hereditary disease. *Lead* was used as a charm against diseases and sorcery. An amulet of *gold* was thought to secure long life. An amulet composed of three threads, one of gold, one of silver, one of iron, was supposed to protect the three vital airs on which the life of the wearer depended. It likewise ensured general protection and prosperity.

In the numerous charms quoted, examples will be given of the employment of most of the above amulets.

Address to an Amulet. II. 17.

1 Power art thou, give me power. All hail!
2 Might art thou, give me might. All hail!
3 Strength art thou, give me strength. All hail!
4 Life art thou, give me life. All hail!
5 Ear art thou, give me hearing. Hail!
6 Eye art thou, give me eyes. All hail!
7 Shield art thou, shield me well. All hail!

The Jangida Plant. XIX. 34.

1 Jangida, thou art Angiras*; thou art a guardian, Jangida.
Let Jangida keep safely all our bipeds and our quadrupeds.
2 Dice-witcheries, the fifty-threes, the hundred witchcraft practisers,
All these may Jangida make weak, bereft of their effectual force.
4 This counteracts the sorceress, this banishes malignity:
Then may victorious Jangida prolong the days we have to live.
7 The ancient plants surpass thee not, nor any herbs of recent days,
A potent charm is Jangida, a most felicitous defence.
9 To thee in truth, O Forest Tree, Indra the mighty One gave strength.
Driving away all maladies, strike thou the demons down, O Plant.
10 Lumbago and rheumatic pain, consumptive cough and pleurisy,
And fever which each autumn brings, may Jangida make powerless.

---

* A great patriarchal Rishi.

An Amulet of Darbha or Kusa Grass. XIX. 29.

1 Pierce thou my rivals, Darbha, pierce the men who fain would fight with me.
Pierce all who wish me evil, pierce the men who hate me, Amulet!
Split, Check, Crush, Shake, Bruise, Burn, Consume, thou my rivals.

9 Slay thou my rivals, Darbha, slay the men who fain would fight with me,
Slay all who wish me evil, slay the men who hate me, Amulet.

Some Amulets are supposed to confer superhuman powers like the Yoga Sastra. The following are examples:

A Charm to obtain Invisibility.—In Hymn 27, Book I. the cast skins of serpents are employed as an amulet to make travellers invisible to robbers.

1 There on the bank those Vipers lie, thrice-seven, having cast their skins:
Now we with their discarded sloughs bind close and cover up the eyes of the malicious highway thief.

A Charm for superhuman Powers of Sight.—In Hymn 20, Book IV. a magical plant, addressed as a goddess, is supposed to enable a person to see every thing in heaven and earth, including demons of all kinds:

1 It sees in front, it sees behind, it sees afar away, it sees
The sky, the firmament, and earth: all this, O Goddess, it beholds.

2 Through thee, O godlike Plant, may I behold all creatures that exist,
Three several heavens, three several earths, and these six regions one by one.

6 Make me see Yátudhánas, make thou Yátudhánís visible.
Make me see all Pisáchas. With this prayer, O Plant, I hold thee fast.

A Charm for Surpassing Strength.—VI. 38.

1 What energy the lion hath, the tiger, adder, and burning fire, Bráhman, or Súrya,
And the blest Goddess who gave birth to Indra, come unto us conjoined with strength and vigour!

2 All energy of elephant and panther, all energy of gold, men, kine, and waters,

3 Might in car, axles, in the strong bull's courage, in Varuna's breath, in Váta, in Parjanya,
In Warrior, in the war drum stretched for battle, in the man's roar, and in the horse's mettle,

COUNTER CHARMS.

It was supposed that the magical incantations of enemies might be rendered powerless or even made to revert upon their own hands. Two examples are given.

Hymn 24, Book II., is a charm against the magic art of demons. Four male demons or sorcerers and four females of the same class are addressed.

1 O Serabhaka, Serabha, back fall your arts of witchery! Back Kimídins! let your weapon fall.
Eat your possessor; eat ye him who sent you forth; eat your own flesh.

&c. &c. &c.

Hymn 18, Book IV. is a counter-charm against the magical incantations of others. A magical plant, gathered at full moon when the night is as day, is employed.

1 The moonlight equalleth the sun, night is the rival of the day.
I make effectual power my help: let magic arts be impotent.

2 Gods! if one make and bring a spell on some man's house who knows it not,
Close as the calf that sucks the cow may it revert and cling to him.

5 I with this Plant have ruined all malignant powers of witchery,
The spell which they have laid upon thy field, thy cattle or thy men.

Charms against Evil Omens.—In ancient times, as at present, the Hindus attached great importance to supposed signs of the success or failure of an undertaking. The lizard bears a high reputation as a prophet, although there is a southern proverb, "The lizard which was the oracle of the whole village has fallen into the broth-pot." The ass appropriately holds a place. Owls and ravens are other guides.

Hymn 64, Books VII. contains a charm to avert an evil omen in which the raven is concerned. Agni Gárhapatya denotes the sacred fire of the householder.

1 From all that woe and trouble may the Waters save and rescue me,
Whate'er the Raven, black of hue, flying out hitherward hath dropped.

2 My Agni Gárhapatya save and set me free from all this guilt
Which the black Raven with thy mouth, O Nirriti,* hath wiped away.

A Charm to avert Evil Omens.—VI. 29.

1 On those men yonder fall the winged missile: the screeching of the Owl is ineffective,
And that the Dove beside the fire hath settled.

---

* Demon of destruction.

2 Thine envoys who came hither, O Destruction, sent or not sent by thee unto our dwelling,
The Dove and Owl, effectless be their visit!

NOTE.—The Owl and Dove were supposed to be birds of evil omen.

CHARMS AGAINST DEMONS.

Even in the times of the Rig-Veda supposed malignant spirits were an object of terror to the Aryans. This feeling was intensified by longer contact with the aborigines, among whom, as throughout a great part of Asia, demonolatry was the prevailing superstition. Sir Monier Williams says:

"The great majority of the inhabitants of India, from the cradle to the burning ground, are haunted and oppressed by a perpetual dread of demons. They are firmly convinced that evil spirits of all kinds, from malignant fiends to merely mischievous imps and elves, are ever on the watch to harm, harass, and torment them, to cause plague, sickness, famine and disaster, to impede, injure, and mar every good work.

"So deep-seated and ineradicable is the fear of evil spirits in the minds of the lower orders, that in many villages of India the doors of the houses are never allowed to face the South, lest the entrance of some dreaded demon should be facilitated."*

The leading demons, male and female, mentioned in the Atharva-Veda will be briefly described:

Arayis.—"One-eyed limping hags."

Asuras.—Evil spirits so called after the giants who fought with the gods.

Dasyus.—Applied both to the wild indigenous races, and to the malignant demons of the air, withholders of the seasonable rain.

Grahi.—A female fiend who seizes men, and causes death and disease.

Kimidins and Kimidinis.—A class of evil spirits whose name is said originally to mean one who goes about crying *Kim idánim.* What now?—a vile and treacherous spy and informer.

Panis.—Demons of darkness who steal the cows of the gods, and shut them up in a cavern,—that is, conceal the rays of daylight in dark clouds.

Pisachas and Pisachis.—General terms for male and female malignant spirits.

Rakshasas and Rakshasis.—Violent and voracious man-eaters.

Yatudhanas and Yatudanis.—A class of evil spirits or sorcerers. Sayana explains them as Rakshasas, but they are apparently distinct.

In Hymn 6, Book VIII., the names of a great many demons are given who attack women; as "the black and hairy Asura,"

---

* *Brahmanism and Hinduism*, pp. 210, 245.

"Snapper and Feeler," "him who eats raw flesh and him who licks his lips;" &c.

Agni and Indra are the two noted "fiend-slayers." Out of about fourteen hymns for the destruction of demons and sorcerers, three are quoted below.

Book I. 28.

1 God Agni hath come forth to us, fiend-slayer, chaser of disease,
Burning the Yátudhánas up, Kimídins, and deceitful ones.
2 Consume the Yátudhánas, God! meet the Kimídins with thy flame:
Burn up the Yátudhánas as they face thee, thou whose path is black!
3 She who hath cursed us with a curse, or hath conceived a murderous sin;
Or seized our son to take his blood, let her devour the child she bare.
4 Let her, the Yátudhání eat son, sister, and her daughter's child.
Now let the Twain* by turns destroy the wild-haired Yátudhánís and crush down Aráyís to the earth!

Book VI. 32.

1 With butter in his hall where fire is burning, perform that sacrifice which quells the goblins.
Burn from afar against the demons, Agni! Afflict not in thy fury us who praise thee.
2 Let Rudra break your necks, O ye Pisáchas, and split your ribs asunder, Yátudhánas!
Here Mitra-Varuna! may we dwell safely: with splendour drive the greedy demons backward.
Let them not find a surety or a refuge, but torn away go down to Death together.

Book VII. 23.

The fearful dream, and indigence, the monster, the malignant hags,
All female fiends of evil name and wicked tongue we drive afar.

CHARMS CONNECTED WITH HOME LIFE.

Picture of Aryan Home Life.—The charms may be fitly introduced by the following graphic sketch by Griffith:

"Setting aside the rivalries, wars and conquests of kings and princes, and the lofty claims and powers of the hierarchy, we may follow the course of the middle-class Aryan's life from the cradle to the funeral pile, and even accompany him to his final home in the world of the Departed.

* Agni and Indra.

"We hear the benedictive charm pronounced over the expectant mother before her child is born, and in due time on the darling's first two teeth. We attend the solemn ceremony in which the youth is invested with his *toga virilis*, the new garment whose assumption signifies his recognition as an adult member of the family with new responsibilities and new duties to perform. As his fancy turns to thoughts of love, we hear him murmuring the charm which shall win him the maiden of his choice, and the lullaby which shall seal every eye but hers in his beloved's house and enable him to visit her without detection or suspicion. We follow him in his formal and somewhat unromantic wooing of a bride through a friend who acts as match-maker; we see the nuptial procession and the bride's introduction to her new home; we hear her benediction on the bridegroom, and the epithalamium pronounced over the wedded pair. The young husband is an agriculturist, and we see him in his field superintending the ploughmen and praying to Indra and Púshan and the Genii of agriculture to bless their labours. Anon, with propitiatory prayer, he is cutting a new channel to bring the water of the brook to the land which is ready for irrigation; or he is praying for rain or an abundant crop. Again, when the corn is ripe, he is busy among the men who gather in the harvest, invoking the aid of the good-natured goblins, and leaving on the ground some sheaves to remunerate their toil. At sunset he superintends the return of the cows who have been grazing under the protection of the Wind-God in the breezy pastures and their return under Divine guidance, and the reunion of all the members of the household are celebrated with symbolical mixt oblation, with milk and a brew of grain.

"His wealth and family increase in answer to his repeated prayer for children and riches, and a new house must be built on a larger scale. The building is erected under the careful eye of the master and blessed and consecrated with prayers to the Gods and to the Queen of the Home. The mistress of the house brings forth the well-filled pitcher, all present are regaled with 'the stream of molten butter blent with nectar—which seems to be a euphemistic name for some sort of good liquor,—and the householder enters and takes formal possession of his new dwelling with fire and water, the two most important necessaries of human life. The house, moreover—a wooden building with a thatched roof—has been specially assured against fire by a prayer to Agni the God of that element with the additional security afforded by the immediate neighbourhood of a good stream or pool of water.

"Such, or something like this, was the ordinary life of the average middle-class agriculturist. A devout believer in the gods, he did not spend his substance on the performance of costly sacrifices, but was content with simple ceremonies and such humble offerings as he could well afford. His chief care was for the health and well-being of himself, his wife, children, and dependents, for plentiful harvests, and for thriving and multiplying cattle; and these were the blessings for which he most frequently prayed. His chief troubles were an occasional touch of malarial fever or rheumatism, a late or scanty rainfall, a storm that lodged his ripe barley, lightning that struck his cattle, and similar mischances caused by the anger of the gods or the malevolence of demons; and he was always armed with prayers and spells against the recurrence of such disasters.

"He was a man of importance in his village, and when he attended the assembly—which may have been a kind of Municipal Committee or Parish Council—his great ambition was to command respect and attention as a speaker, and with this view he fortified himself with charm and magic herb that inspired eloquence, and enabled him to overpower his opponents in debate. His life, on the whole, was somewhat monotonous and dull, but it seems to have suited him as he was continually praying that it might be extended to its full natural duration of a hundred years. At the end of that time, with his sons and his sons' children around him, he was ready to pass away to the felicity that awaited him in the world of the Fathers.

The small merchant or trader lived a less settled life and saw more of the world than the agriculturist. We see him on the point of starting on a journey for business purposes with his little stock of goods. He first propitiates Indra who as a merchant also, the God who trades and traffics with his worshippers, requiring and receiving prayer and oblations in exchange for the blessings which he sends, and who will now free the travelling merchant's path from wild beasts, robbers, and enemies of every kind. He prays also to many other deities that he may make a rich profit and gain a hundred treasures, and commits the care of his children and cattle in his absence to Agni, the God of all Aryan men. His ritual is an extensive one as he may be about to journey to all points of the compass, and he must accordingly conciliate all the divine Warders of the heavenly regions. He has to recite some ten hymns of Book VI. invoking the aid of all protecting deities, not forgetting to consult the Weather-Prophet, and to obtain from him the promise of auspicious mornings, noons, and nights. He bids an affectionate farewell to the houses of his village, and departs on his way encouraged by the hymn which ensures him a safe and successful journey. In due time he returns having bartered his wares for the treasures of distant places, for bdellium and other fragrant gums and unguents, for Kushtha and other foreign plants and drugs of healing virtue, for mother-of-pearl, ornaments for the women, and perhaps cloth of finer wool.

"The merchant's object in life is gain, and he is not always very scrupulous in his dealings. If he is in debt he would prefer to be freed by the intervention of a god, and not by his own exertions; and he is bold enough even to pray for release from debts which he has incurred without intending to pay them. He is probably the gambler who prays for success in play, and for pardon when he has been guilty of cheating." *Preface*, pp. IX.-XIII.

CHARMS CONNECTED WITH FAMILY LIFE.

A Man's Love Charms.

There are seven hymns entitled, "A Man's Love Charms." They show that infant marriage did not prevail in Vedic times.

A Charm to win a Maiden's Love. VI. 8.

1 Like as the creeper throws her arms on every side around the tree,
So hold thou me in thine embrace that thou mayst be in love with me, my darling, never to depart.

2 As, when he mounts, the eagle strikes his pinions downward on the earth,
So do I strike thy spirit down that thou mayst be in love with me, my darling, never to depart.
3 As in his rapid course the Sun encompasses the heaven and earth,
So do I compass round thy mind that thou mayst be in love with me, my darling, never to depart.

A Charm to win a Bride. VI. 82.

1 I call the name of him who comes, hath come, and still draws nigh to us.
Foe-slaying Indra's name I love, the Vasus' friend with hundred powers.
2 Thus Bhaga spake to me : Let him bring thee a consort by the path.
Whereon the Asvins brought the bride Súryá, the child of Savitar.
3 Great, Indra, is that hook of thine, bestowing treasure, wrought of gold :
Therewith, O Lord of Might, bestow a wife on me who long to wed.

NOTE.—The Asvins are said to have obtained Súryá, daughter of the Sun, as a wife for Soma, the Moon-God.

A Sleep Charm of a Lover who is secretly visiting his Love. IV. 5.

1 The Bull who hath a thousand horns, who rises up from out the sea,—
By him the strong and mighty one we lull the folk to rest and sleep.
2 Over the surface of the earth there breathes no wind, there looks no eye.
Lull all the women, lull the dogs to sleep, with Indra as thy friend !
3 The women sleeping in the court, lying without, or stretched on beds,
The matrons with their odorous sweets—these, one and all, we lull to sleep.
6 Sleep mother, let the father sleep, sleep dog, and master of the home.
Let all her kinsmen sleep, sleep all the people who are round about.
7 With soporific charm, O Sleep, lull thou to slumber all the folk,
Let the rest sleep till break of day, I will remain awake till dawn, like Indra free from scath and harm.

NOTE.—The *Bull* is variously supposed to mean the sun, the starry heavens, or the moon.

Charm for the safe delivery of a Son. VI. 81.

1 Thou art a grasper, holding fast both hands ; thou drivest fiends away.
A holder both of progeny and riches hath this Ring become.

2 Prepare accordantly, O Ring, the mother for the infant's birth.
On the right way bring forth the boy. Make him come hither. I am here.

3 The Amulet which Aditi wore when desirous of a son,
Tvashtar hath bound upon this dame and said, Be mother of a boy.

Benediction on a new-born child. VI. 110.

1 Yea, ancient, meet for praise at sacrifices, ever and now thou sittest down as Hotar.
And now, O Agni, make thy person friendly, and win felicity for us by worship.

2 'Neath Jyaishthaghnî and Yama's Two Releasers this child was born: preserve him from uprooting.
He shall conduct him safe past all misfortunes to lengthened life that lasts a hundred autumns.

3 Born on the Tiger's day was he, a hero, the Constellation's child, born brave and manly.
Let him not wound, when grown in strength, his father, nor disregard his mother, her who bare him.

NOTES.—A hymn to Agni. *Jyaishthaghnî*: the 16th lunar mansion. *Yama's two Releasers*: two auspicious stars whose rising releases from Death and disease. The *Tiger* is in the Atharva-Veda the type of valour.

A Blessing on a Child's first two Teeth. VI. 140.

1 Two tigers have grown up who long to eat the mother and the sire:
Soothe, Brahmanaspati, and thou, O Játavedas, both these teeth.

2 Let rice and barley be your food, eat also beans and sesamum,
This is the share allotted you, to be your portion, ye two Teeth. Harm not your mother and your sire.

3 Both fellow-teeth have been invoked, gentle and bringing happiness.
Elsewhither let the fierceness of your nature turn away, O Teeth! harm not your mother or your sire.

A Youth's Investiture with a new Garment. II. 13.

1 Strength-giver, winning lengthened life, O Agni, with face, and back shining with molten butter,
Drink thou the butter and fair milk and honey, and, as a sire his sons, keep this man safely.

2 For us surround him, cover him with splendour, give him long life, and death when age removes him,
The garment hath Brihaspati presented to Soma, to the King, to wrap about him.

3 Thou for our weal hast clothed thee in the mantle: thou hast become our heifers' guard from witchcraft.
Live thou a hundred full and plenteous autumns, and wrap thee in prosperity of riches.

4 Come hither, stand upon the stone: thy body shall become a stone,
The Universal Gods shall make thy life a hundred autumns long.
5 So may the Universal Gods protect thee, whom we divest of raiment worn aforetime.
So after thee, well-formed and growing stronger, be born a multitude of thriving brothers.

Marriage Ceremonies.

These are described under Hymns about Women.

Benediction on the Completion of a New Home. III. 12.

1 Here even here I fix my firm-set dwelling; flowing with fatness may it stand in safety.
May we approach thee, House! with all our people; unharmed and goodly men, and dwell within thee.
3 A spacious store, O House, art thou, full of clean corn and lofty-roofed.
Let the young calf and little boy approach thee, and milch-kine streaming homeward in the evening.
4 This House may Savitar and Váyu stablish, Brihaspati who knows the way, and Indra.
May the moist Maruts sprinkle it with fatness, and may King Bhaga make our corn-land fruitful.
8 Bring hitherward, O dame, the well-filled pitcher, the stream, of molten butter blent with nectar.
Bedew these drinkers with a draught of Amrit. May all our hopes' fulfilment guard this dwelling.
9 Water that kills Consumption, free from all Consumption here I bring.
With Agni, the immortal One, I enter and possess the house.

Agricultural Labours.

Several charms refers to these—a few of which may be quoted.

A Farmer's song to speed the Plough. III. 17.

1 Wise and devoted to the gods, the skilful men bind ploughropes fast,
And lay the yokes on either side.
6 Happily work our steers and men! May the plough furrow happily.
Happily be the traces bound. Happily ply the driving-goad.
8 Auspicious Sítá, come thou near; we venerate and worship thee
That thou mayst bless and prosper us and bring us fruits abundantly.
9 Loved by the Visvedevas and the Maruts, let Sétá be bedewed with oil and honey.
Turn thou to us with wealth of milk, O Sita, in vigorous strength and pouring streams of fatness.

A Charm to hasten the coming of the Rains.

After the long hot season when the earth is as iron, the coming of the rains is eagerly desired. Indra or Parjanya was especially worshipped as able, with his thunderbolts, to cleave the rain-clouds and compel them to let fall their treasures. Some verses from Hymn 15, Book IV. are quoted below:

1 Let all the misty regions fly together, let all the rain-clouds sped by wind, assemble.
Let waters satisfy the earth, the voices of the great mist-envelop-ed Bull who roareth.

8 Let lightning flash on every side; from all the regions blow the winds!
Urged by the Maruts let the clouds pour down their rain upon the earth.

13 They who lay quiet for a year, the Brahmans who fulfil their vows,
The frogs, have lifted up their voice, the voice Parjanya hath inspired.

16 Lift up the mighty cask, and pour down water; let the wind blow and lightning flash around us.
Let sacrifice be paid, and, widely scattered, let herbs and plants be full of joy and gladness.

NOTES.—The *Bull*: Parjanya, god of the rain-cloud. Verse 13 is taken from Rig-Veda, vii. 103. The frogs rejoicing in the rains are represented as Brahmans engaged in religious ceremonies. *Cask*: rain-cloud.

A Charm to protect corn from Lightning and Drought.

BOOK VII. 11.

That far-spread thunder, sent from thee, which cometh on all this world, a high celestial signal—
Strike not, O God, our growing corn with lightning, nor kill it with the burning rays of Súrya.

CHARMS TO PROTECT CATTLE.

Both oxen and cows occupy a prominent place in the Atharva-Veda. Hymn 25, Book xix is a charm to be used when a young ox is yoked for the first time. Hymn 16, Book V. contains a charm for the increase of cattle. Hymn 21, Book IV. is a glorification and benediction addressed to cows. Hymn 59, Book VI., quoted below, is a charm, addressed to Arundhati, to protect cattle and men.

Hymn 32, Book II, is a charm against the worms which infest cows. Hymn 77 Book VI is a charm to bring the cattle home, and Hymn 14, Book III. is a benediction of the cattle-pen, in which the cows are kept at night.

1 First, O Arundhatí, protect our oxen and our milky kine:
Protect each one that is infirm, each quadruped that yields no milk.
2 Let the Plant give us sheltering aid, Arundhatí allied with gods,
Avert consumption from our men and make our cow-pen rich in milk.
3 I welcome the auspicious Plant, life-giving, wearing every hue,
Far from our cattle may it turn the deadly dart which Rudra casts.

Charm to make a Cow love its Calf. VI. 70.

This might seem a work of supererogation; but the Aryan knew better. Bloomfield, in his commentary, describes how it was used:

"The practice consists in washing the calf, sprinkling it with the cow's urine, leading it thrice around the cow and tying it near her while the hymn is being recited. It is then recited once more over the head and ears of the calf." p. 493.

1. As wine associates with flesh, as dice attend the gaming-board,
As an enamoured man's desire is firmly set upon a dame,
So let thy heart and soul, O Cow, be firmly set upon thy calf.
&c., &c.

Charm for the destruction of Vermin. VI. 50.

1 Destroy the rat, the mole, the boring beetle, cut off their heads and crush their ribs, O Asvins.
Bind fast their mouths; let them not eat our barley; so guard, ye twain, our growing corn from danger.
3 Hearken to me, lord of the female borer, lord of the female grub! ye rough-toothed vermin!
Whate'er ye be, dwelling in woods, and piercing, we crush and mangle all those piercing insects.

Charm for a Plentiful Harvest. VI. 142.

1 Spring high, O Barley, and become much through thine own magnificence:
Burst all the vessels; let the bolt from heaven forbear to strike thee down.
2 As we invite and call to thee, Barley, a God who heareth us,
Raise thyself up like heaven on high, and be exhaustless as the sea.
3 Exhaustless let thine out-turns be, exhaustless be thy gathered heaps,
Exhaustless be thy givers, and exhaustless those who eat of thee.

Song of Harvest Home. III. 24.

5 O Hundred-handed, gather up. O Thousand-handed, pour thou forth.
Bring hither increase of the corn prepared and yet to be prepared.

5

6 Three sheaves are the Gandharvas' claim, the lady of the house hath four.
We touch thee with the sheaf that is the most abundant of them all.
7 Adding and Gathering are thy two attendants, O Prajápati.
May they bring hither increase, wealth abundant, inexhaustible.

NOTE.—Three sheaves were left on the ground for the demons who are here called Gandharvas, a higher class of celestial beings; four sheaves were for the mistress; and the best of all is offered as a sample to the owner of the field.

Miscellaneous Charms connected with Home Life.

Prayer for Wealth and Children.

These form the most frequent petitions.

Book VII. 17.

1 May the Ordainer give us wealth, Lord, ruler of the world of life: with full hand may he give to us.
2 May Dhátar grant the worshipper henceforth inperishable life,
May we obtain the favour of the God who giveth every boon.
3 To him may Dhátar grant all kinds of blessings who, craving children, serves him in his dwelling.
Him may the Gods invest with life eternal, yea, all the gods and Aditi accordant.
4 May this our gift please Savitar, Ráti, Dhátar, Prajápati, and Agni, Lord of Treasures,
May Tvashtar, Vishnu, blessing him with children, give store of riches to the sacrificer.

NOTE.—*Ráti*, the gift personified as a goddess.

The Hospitable Reception of Guests. IX. 6.

This is a long prose hymn in which the hospitable reception of guests is regarded as identical with sacrifice offered to the gods. Only a few verses can be quoted:

19 When he says, Bring out more, he lengthens his life thereby.
25 This man whose food they eat hath all his wickedness blotted out. 26. All that man's sin whose food they do not eat remains unblotted out.
28 The arranged sacrifice of the man who offers food is a sacrifice to Prajápati. 29. The man who offers food follows the steps of Prajápati.

A Charm to win Love in a Family. III. 30.

1 Freedom from hate I bring to you, concord and unanimity.
Love one another as the cow loveth the calf that she hath borne.
2 One-minded with his mother let the son be loyal to his sire.
Let the wife, calm and gentle, speak words sweet as honey to her lord.
3 No brother hate his brother, no sister to sister be unkind.
Unanimous, with one intent, speak ye your speech in friendliness.

4 That spell through which gods sever not, nor ever bear each other hate,
That spell we lay upon your home, a bond of union for the men.

. . . . . .

7 With binding charm I make you all united, obeying one sole leader and one-minded.
Even as the gods who watch and guard the Amrit, at morn and eve may ye be kindly-hearted.

Hymn 42, Book III. is a "Charm to reconcile estranged Friends."

A Charm for Influence at a Meeting. VII. 12.

1 In concord may Prajápati's two daughters, Gathering and Assembly, both protect me.
May every man I meet respect and aid me. Fair be my words, O Fathers, at the meetings.
2 Let all the company who join the Conference agree with me.
3 Indra, make me conspicuous in all this gathered company.

Hymn 27, Book II. is a charm against an opponent in a debate.

A Merchant's Prayer for Success in Business.

The prayer is primarily addressed to the "Merchant Indra," for reasons which have already been stated. Vaisvánara and Játavedas are epithets applied to Agni.

Book III. 15.

1 I stir and animate the merchant Indra: may he approach and be our guide and leader.
Chasing ill-will, wild beast, and highway robber, may he who hath the power give me riches.
2 The many paths which gods are wont to travel, the paths which go between the earth and heaven,
May they rejoice with me in milk and fatness that I may make rich profit by my purchase.
3 With fuel, Agni! and with butter, longing, mine offering I present for strength and conquest;
With prayer, so far as I have strength, adoring—this holy hymn to gain a hundred treasures.
4 Pardon this stubbornness of ours, O Agni, the distant pathway which our feet have trodden.
Propitious unto us be sale and barter, may interchange of merchandise enrich me.
Accept, ye twain, accordant, this libation! Prosperous be our ventures and incomings.
5 The wealth wherewith I carry on my traffic, seeking, ye gods! wealth with the wealth I offer,
May this grow more for me, not less: O Agni, through sacrifice chase those away who hinder profit!

6 The wealth wherewith I carry on my traffic, seeking, ye gods! wealth with the wealth I offer,
Herein may Indra, Savitar, and Soma, Prajápati and Agni give me splendour.
7 With reverence we sing thy praise, O Hotar-priest Vaisvánara.
Over our children keep thou watch, over our bodies, kine, and lives.
8 Still to thee ever will we bring oblation, as to a stabled horse, O Játavedas.
Joying in food and in the growth of riches may we thy servants, Agni, never suffer.

MISCELLANEOUS HYMNS.

Several hymns will now be noticed which vary in character.

Hymns about Kings.

There are some hymns about the election of a King, the consecration of a King, the benediction of a King, the restoration of a King, a King's address to an amulet which is to strengthen his authority; a King's charm to secure the fidelity of his people; a charm to reconcile a King's discontented people. There is even a charm to tame an elephant for a King.

One specimen is given.

A Benediction on a newly consecrated King. IV. 22.

1. Exalt and strengthen this my Prince, O Indra. Make him sole lord and leader of the people.
Scatter his foes, deliver all his rivals into his hand in struggles for precedence.
2. Give him a share in village, kine, and horses, and leave his enemy without a portion.
Let him as King be head and chief of Princes. Give up to him, O Indra, every foeman. &c., &c.

Charms for success in War and the Destruction of Enemies.

Hymns are addressed to the chariot and war-drum as charms to secure victory over enemies; there are imprecations against a hostile army, &c. A few quotations are made.

A Charm to secure success in Battle. III. 1.

1 Let the wise Agni go against our foemen, burning against ill-will and imprecation.
Let him bewilder our opponents' army. Let Játevedas smite and make them handless.

4 Shot down the slope, with thy two tawny coursers, forth go thy bolt, destroying foes, O Indra!
Slay those who fly, slay those who stand and follow.
On every side fulfil these men's intention.
6 Let Indra daze their army. Let the Maruts slay it with their might.
Let Agni take their eyes away, and let the conquered host retreat.

NOTE.—The hymn was supposed to have magical effect in bewildering an enemy.

Charms for the Destruction of Enemies.

BOOK IV. 36.

1 Endowed with true strength, let the Bull, Agni Vaisvánara, burn them up,
Him who would pain and injure us, him who would treat us as a foe.
2 Him who, unharmed, would injure us, and him who, harmed, would do us harm,
I lay between the doubled fangs of Agni, of Vaisvánara.

BOOK VII. 59.

Like a tree struck by lightning may the man be withered from the root,
Who curseth us who curse him not, or, when we curse him, curseth us.

BOOK XIX. 29.

1 Pierce thou my rivals, Darbha, pierce the men who fain would fight with me.
Pierce all who wish me evil, pierce the men who hate me, Amulet.
9 Slay thou my rivals, Darbha, slay the men who fain would fight with me.
Slay all who wish me evil, slay the men who hate me, Amulet.

HYMNS ON BRAHMANS.

The four castes are only once mentioned in the Rig-Veda in one of the latest hymns. By the time the Atharva-Veda was collected, caste had been largely developed. There are numerous references to Brahmans and Kshatriyas, and the rights of the former are carefully guarded.

Two hymns about Brahmans are partly quoted:

The Duty of giving cows to Brahmans, and the Danger of withholding them. XII. 4.

1 I give the gift, shall be his word; and straightway they have bound the Cow.
For Brahman priests who beg the boon. That bringeth sons and progeny.

10 For gods and Brahmans is the Cow produced when first she springs to life,
Hence to the priests must she be given: this they call guarding private wealth.
25 The Cow deprives of progeny and makes him poor in cattle who Retains in his possession her whom Brahmans have solicited.

The Sin and Danger of Robbing a Brahman of his Cow.

In Hymn 5, Book XII., this is shown at great length. Only a few verses are quoted. The consequences are terrific:

5 Of the Kshatriya who taketh to himself this Brahman's cow and oppresseth the Brahman,
The glory, the heroism, and the favouring fortune depart.
67 Strike off the shoulders and the head.
68 Snatch thou the hair from off his head, and from his body strip the skin:
69 Tear out his sinews, cause his flesh to fall in pieces from his frame.
70 Crush thou his bones together, strike and beat the marrow out of him.
71 Dislocate all his limbs and joints.
72 From earth let the carnivorous Agni drive him, let Váyu burn him from mid-air's broad region,
73 From heaven let Súrya drive him and consume him.

In Hymn 18, Book V., a Kshatriya is warned against the sin of eating a Brahman's cow. In the preceding hymn, taken partly from Rig-Veda X. 109, an account is given of the abduction by a Kshatriya of a Brahman's wife and her subsequent restoration to her husband. Hymn 19, Book V., is on the wickedness and ruinous consequences of oppressing, robbing, or insulting a Brahman.

Hymns about Debt.

The Indian tendency to run into debt is of long standing. In the Rig-Veda a prayer is addressed to Varuna for freedom from debt. The following, in the Atharva-Veda, is of the same character.

Book VI. 117.

1 That which I eat, a debt which is still owing, the tribute due to Yama, which supports me,
Thereby may I be free from debt, O Agni. Thou knowest how to rend all bonds asunder.
3 May we be free in this world and that yonder, in the third world may we be unindebted.
May we, debt-free, abide in all the pathways, in all the worlds which Gods and Fathers visit.

Release from Debts incurred without intention of Payment.

Agni is asked to aid the suppliant in the dishonest attempt to break his promise, and get rid of debts contracted without intention of repayment. Agni knows how to tear to pieces the bonds of debt. Thus the creditor's hopes of payment would be disappointed.

Book VI. 119.

1 The debt which I incur, not gaming, Agni! and, not intending to repay, acknowledge,
That may Vaisvánara, the best, our sovran, carry away into the world of virtue.
2 I cause Vaisvánara to know, confessing the debt whose payment to the gods is promised.
He knows to tear asunder all these nooses: so may we dwell with him the gentle-minded.
3 Vaisvánara the Purifier purge me when I oppose their hope and break my promise,
Unknowing in my heart. With supplication, whatever guilt there is in that, I banish.

In Hymn 117, Book VI. the petitioner prays for release from debt, both in this world and in the next. Newcomers in heaven were expected to pay one-sixteenth of their merit to Yama; but they might compound for it by a sacrifice on earth.

Hymns on Gambling.

In the Rig-Veda a gambler bewails the results of his folly. The following two hymns are from the Atharva-Veda.

A Charm for success in Gambling. IV. 38.

1 Hither I call the Apsaras, victorious, who plays with skill,
Her who comes freely forth to view, who wins the stakes in games of dice.
3 Dancing around us with the dice, winning the wager by her play,
May she obtain the stake for us and gain the victory with skill.
May she approach us full of strength; let them not win this wealth of ours.

Notes.—The Apsarases, the wives of the Gandharvas, were supposed to be fond of gambling and able to influence the gambler's luck.

A Prayer asking forgiveness for cheating at Play. VI. 118.

1 If we have sinned with both our hands, desiring to take the host of dice for our possession,
May both Apsarases to-day forgive us that debt, the fiercely-conquering, fiercely-looking.
2 Stern viewers of their sins who rule the people, forgive us what hath happened as we gambled.
Not urging us to pay the debt we owed him, he with a cord hath gone to Yama's kingdom.

Note.—*With a cord:* to keep us bound as debtors in the other world.

SELECTIONS FROM FUNERAL HYMNS.

Book XVIII. contains four Hymns relating to funeral rites and sacrificial offerings to the Pitris. They are nearly all taken from the Rig-Veda Book X., with variations. They begin with a dialogue between Yama and his twin sister Yami, the first human pair, the originators of the race. Yami at first declines the request of Yama to make her his wife. A few quotations are given.

Address to the spirit of the Dead Man. XVIII. 1.

54 Go forth, go forth upon the homeward pathways whither our sires of old have gone before us.
There shalt thou look on both the Kings enjoying their sacred food, God Varuna and Yama.

Hymn 2.

55 Lord of all life, let Ayu (Váyu) guard thee, Púshan convey thee forward on the distant pathway.
May Savitar the God conduct thee thither where dwell the pious who have gone before thee.

Hymn 3.

58 Meet Yama, meet the Fathers, meet the merit of virtuous action in the loftiest heaven.
Leave sin and evil, seek anew thy dwelling: so bright with glory let him join his body.
73 Mount to this life, removing all defilement: here thine own kindred shine with lofty splendour.
Depart thou; be not left behind: go forward, first of those here, unto the world of Fathers.

Address to Agni. XVIII. 2.

10 Away, O Agni, to the Pitris send him who, offered in thee, goes with our oblations.
Wearing new life, let him approach his offspring, and splendid, be invested with a body.

Address to Yama. XVIII. 2.

12 And those two dogs of thine, Yama, the watchers, four-eyed who look on men and guard the pathway,
Entrust this man, O King, to their protection, and with prosperity and health endow him.

Address to the Dead Husband. XVIII. 3.

1 Choosing her husband's world, O man, this woman lays herself down beside thy lifeless body,
Preserving faithfully the ancient custom. Bestow upon her here both wealth and offspring.

Address to the Widow. XVIII. 3.

2 Rise, come unto the world of life, O woman; come, he is lifeless by whose side thou liest.
Wifehood with this thy husband was thy portion, who took thy hand and wooed thee as a lover.

It was an ancient custom among the Aryans before they entered India for the widow to be burned with the dead body of her husband. The widow in the hymn is supposed to lie down by the corpse on the funeral pile; but the husband's brother or some old friend makes her leave the body of the dead.

The second verse was mistranslated by the Brahmans to encourage widow burning, leading to untold deaths, that they might be enriched by the offerings on the occasion.

Worship of Yama. XVIII. 3.

13 Worship with sacrificial gift King Yama, Vivasván's son who gathers men together,
Yama who was the first to die of mortals, the first who travelled to the world before us.

Address to the Pitris. XVIII. 3.

44 Fathers whom Agni's flames have tasted, come ye nigh: in perfect order take ye each your proper place.
Eat sacrificial food presented on the grass: grant riches with a multitude of hero sons.

Address to the Earth on the burial of the Remains. XVIII. 3.

49 Betake thee to the lap of Earth, our mother, of Earth far-spreading, very kind and gracious.
May she, wool-soft unto the guerdon-giver, guard thee in front upon the distant pathway.
50 Heave, thyself, Earth, nor press him downward heavily: afford him easy access, pleasant to approach.
Cover him as a mother wraps her skirt about her child, O Earth!

CHARMS ABOUT WOMEN.

The hymns on home life often refer to women. To point out more clearly the feeling regarding them, a few are quoted, supposed to be spoken by women themselves, or with which they are more specially concerned.

A Maiden's Love Charm. VII. 38.

The reference is to a plant whose powers are thus described:

1 I dig this healing Herb that makes my lover look on me and weep;
That bids the parting friend return and kindly greets him as he comes.

2 With this same Herb I draw thee, close that I may be most dear to thee.
4 Thou shalt be mine and only mine, and never mention other dames.
5 If thou art far away beyond the rivers, far away from men,
This Herb shall seem to bind thee fast and bring thee back my prisoner.

A Woman's Love Charm. VI. 130.

1 This is the Apsarases' love-spell, the conquering resistless ones'.
Send the spell forth, ye Deities! Let him consume with love of me.
2 I pray, may he remember me, think of me, loving and beloved.
Send forth the spell, ye Deities! let him consume with love of me.
3 That he may think of me, that I may never, never think of him,
Send forth the spell, ye Deities! Let him consume with love of me.
4 Madden him, Maruts, madden him. Madden him, madden him, O Air.
Madden him, Agni, madden him. Let him consume with love of me.

A Charm to Win a Husband. VI. 60.

1 With forelock loosened o'er his brow here comes the wooer of the bride,
Seeking a husband for this maid, a wife for this unmarried man.
2 Wooer! this girl hath toiled in vain, going to others' marriages.
Now to her wedding, verily, wooer! another maid shall come.
3 Dhátar upholds the spacious earth, upholds the sky, upholds the Sun.
Dhátar bestow upon this maid a husband suited to her wish!

NOTES:—The *wooer* is the matchmaker whose business it is to arrange marriages. *Dhátar* is regarded as the upholder of the sacrament of marriage.

Hymn 36, Book II. is a charm to secure a husband for a marriageable girl.

MARRIAGE CEREMONIES.

A Nuptial Benediction. VI. 78.

1 Let this man be again bedewed with this presented sacrifice,
And comfort with the sap of life the bride whom they have brought to him.
2 With life's sap let him comfort her, and raise her high with princely sway.
In wealth that hath a thousand powers, this pair be inexhaustible!
3 Tvashtar formed her to be thy dame, Tvashtar made thee to be her lord.
Long life let Tvashtar give you both. Let Tvashtar give a thousand lives.

A nuptial Charm spoken by the Bride. VII. 37.

With this my robe, inherited from Manu, I envelop thee,
So that thou mayst be all mine own and give no thought to other dames.

A Charm to be pronounced by Bride and Bridegroom. VII. 36.

Sweet are the glances of our eyes, our faces are as smooth as balm.
Within thy bosom harbour me; one spirit dwell in both of us!

NOTE.—The pair anoint each other's eyes as part of the marriage ceremony.

Dignity of the Bride. XIV. 1.

43 As vigorous Sindhu won himself imperial lordship of the streams,
So be imperial queen when thou hast come within thy husband's home.

44 Over thy husband's fathers and his brothers be imperial queen,
Over thy husband's sister and his mother bear supreme control.

Gentleness enjoined on the Bride. XIV. 2.

This shows conclusively that the bride was not a child subject to her mother-in-law.

26 Bliss-bringer, furthering thy household's welfare, dear, gladdening thy husband and his father, enter this home, mild to thy husband's mother.

27 Be pleasant to thy husband's sire, sweet to thy household and thy lord.
To all this clan be gentle, and favour these men's prosperity.

A Charm against Sterility and to assure the birth of Male Children. III. 23.

Barrenness is what a wife most dreads. The birth of a son will best secure her position.

1 From thee we banish and expel the cause of thy sterility.
This in another place we lay apart from thee and far removed.

2 As arrow to the quiver, so let a male embryo enter thee.
Then from thy side be born a babe, a ten-month child, thy hero son.

3 Bring forth a male, bring forth a son. Another male shall follow him.
The mother shalt thou be of sons born and hereafter to be born.

6 May those celestial herbs whose sire was Heaven, the Earth their mother, and their root the ocean,
May those celestial healing Plants assist thee to obtain a son.

The Birth of a Daughter Deprecated. VI. 11.

1 Asvattha on the Samí-tree. There a male birth is certified.
There is the finding of a son: this bring we to the women-folk.

2 The father sows the genial seed, the woman tends and fosters it.
This is the finding of a son: thus hath Prajápati declared.
3 Prajápati, Anumati, Sinívâlí have ordered it.
Elsewhere may he effect the birth of maids, but here prepare a boy.

NOTE.—The Asvattha, masculine, growing on the Samí-tree, feminine, is typical of a male child. Prajápati, Lord of life, was invoked on such occasions. Anumati and Sinívâlí were deities presiding over childbirth.

Charms against Jealousy.

Hymn 45, Book VII. contains a Charm to "calm a lover's Jealousy." Hymn 18, Book VI., "A Charm to banish Jealousy," is quoted below:

1 The first approach of Jealousy, and that which followeth the first,
The pain, the fire that burns within thy heart, we quench and drive away.
2 Even as the earth is dead to sense, yea, more unconscious than the dead,
Even as a corpse's spirit is the spirit of the jealous man.
3 The thought that harbours in thy heart, the fluttering doubt that dwells therein,
Yea, all thy jealousy, like heat born of the dance, I banish thence.

Imprecation on an Unfaithful Lover. VI. 138.

1 O Plant, thy fame is spread abroad as best of all the herbs that grow.
Unman for me to-day this man that he may wear the horn of hair.
2 Make him a eunuch with a horn, set thou the crest upon his head.
Let Indra with two pressing-stones deprive him of his manly strength.
3 I have unmanned thee, eunuch! yea, impotent! made thee impotent, and robbed thee, weakling! of thy strength.
Upon his head we set the horn, we set the branching ornament.

NOTES.—*The horn of hair*, regarded as a mark of effeminacy. Verses 4 & 5 are so indecent as to be untranslatable in English.

A Spell to rid a jealous wife of a more favoured Rival. III. 18.

Polygamy seems to have prevailed to some extent. Book VII. contains two Hymns, Nos. 113, 114; with spells of this description. Hymn 18, Book III is quoted below:

1 From out the earth I dig this Plant, an herb of most effectual power,
Wherewith one quells the rival wife, and gains the husband for one's self.

2 Auspicious, with expanded leaves, sent by the Gods, victorious Plant,
Drive thou the rival wife away, and make my husband only mine.
3 Indeed he hath not named her name; thou with this husband dalliest not.
Far into distance most remote we drive the rival wife away.
4 Stronger am I, O stronger one, yea, mightier than the mightier;
Beneath me be my rival wife, down, lower than the lowest dames!
5 I am the conqueror, and thou, thou also art victorious:
As victory attends us both we will subdue my fellow-wife.
6 I've girt thee with the conquering Plant, beneath thee laid the mightiest one.
As a cow hastens to her calf, so let thy spirit speed to me, hasten like water on its way.

NOTE.—The hymn is taken, with variations, from Rig-Veda X. 145. The plant is supposed to be a climbing plant, employed for magical purposes.

Incantation against evil spirits that beset women.— Hymn 16, Book XIV. gives a long account of demons supposed to molest women.

THE GODS OF THE ATHARVA-VEDA.

The deities invoked are much the same as in the Rig-Veda. The principal will be briefly noticed, with illustrative quotations.

Agni.—This god, to whom the first hymn of the Rig-Veda is addressed, occupies the foremost place in the Atharva-Veda. There are more references to him than to any other deity. He is addressed in his various forms. He is ordinary fire, the sacred household fire. A prayer is offered to him to protect a house against fire. As lightning, Agni springs from the clouds. He is repeatedly invoked as the Sun. Agni is the fiend-slayer, the special tutelary deity of the five tribes of Aryan men; the giver of wealth, the giver of children; the lord of the seasons. He is the Hotar priest, the sacrificer. Lastly, as flesh-consumer, he is the fire of the funeral pile.

Játavedas, the wise, the sapient, and *Vaisvánara*, belonging to all (Aryan) men, universal;—are two epithets frequently applied to Agni.

Hymn 64, Book XIX., quoted below, is a prayer to Agni for children and long life, which he is asked to give in return for the wood burnt in his honour.

1 For lofty Játavedas I have brought the fuel hither first.
May he who knoweth all bestow faith and intelligence on me.
2 With fuel and with flaming wood we, Játavedas, strengthen thee;
So do thou strengthen us in turn with children and with store of wealth.
3 Whatever even be the logs which, Agni, we lay down for thee,
Propitious be it all to me: accept it, O most youthful God.

4 Agni, these logs are thine; with these be, fain to burn! a flaming brand.
Vouchsafe us length of life and give us hope of immortality.

Hymn 21, Book III. in honour of all varieties of fire, is especially a charm to appease Agni in his most dreaded form, and to quench the flames of the funeral pile. It ends as follows:

4 The all-devouring God whom men call Káma, he whom they call the Giver and Receiver,
Invincible, pervading, wise, and mighty—to all these Fires be this oblation offered.

Indra.—As in the Rig-Veda, Indra occupies a very prominent place. The references to him are next in number to those of Agni. Numerous epithets are applied to him; as the Soma-drinker, the Fiend-slayer, the Mighty Bull, the Conqueror, the Thunderer, the Destroyer, the Giver of Bliss, &c. He is invoked with his thunderbolts, to put to flight the demons of the air and set free the rain, that it may descend in torrents. Alone, or in conjunction with Agni, he is asked to destroy all other demons. His aid is likewise specially solicited in battle, for success against enemies. Plenteous wealth, long life, and numerous sons are other gifts which he is asked to bestow.

As already mentioned, the whole of Book XX., with the exception of the Kuntápa section, is almost exclusively devoted to the praise of Indra. Both it and other hymns to Indra are mostly taken from the Rig-Veda.

Hymn 8, Book XX., in praise of Indra, is as follows:

1 Drink as of old, and let the draught delight thee:
Hear thou my prayer and let our songs exalt thee.
Make the Sun visible, make food abundant: slaughter the foes, pierce through and free the cattle.

2 Come to us; they have called thee Soma-lover.
Here is the pressed juice, drink thereof for rapture.
Widely-capacious, pour it down within thee, and invocated hear us like a father.

8 Full is his chalice. Blessing! Like a pourer I have filled up the vessel for his drinking,
Presented on the right, dear Soma juices have brought us Indra, to rejoice him, hither.

NOTES.—Taken from Rig-Veda. *The cattle,* the clouds which are to be dispersed.

Heaven and Earth.—Dyaus, heaven, denotes the bright sky itself, the old Dyaus, worshipped as we know by the Aryans before they broke up into separate peoples, and languages, and surviving in Greece as Zeus, in Italy as Jupiter, and among the Teutonic nations as *Tyr* or Tiu.*

* *India: What can it teach us?* p. 194.

Prithivi, the Earth, literally 'the wide,' 'the extended,' was early associated with Dyaus. Originally they were closely united. In Rig-Veda 1. 67 Agni is said to have separated them and fixed them in their present position; but in other parts of the Rig-Veda this action is ascribed to Indra, to Varuna, to Soma, etc. Lang says in *Custom and Myth*, that this old surviving nature myth of the original union and subsequent forcible separation of heaven and earth is found in Greece, China, and New Zealand, as well as in India.

There are numerous reference to Heaven and Earth personified in the Atharva-Veda. In Hymn 26, Book IV. the refrain is:

Deliver us, ye twain, from grief and trouble.

Hymn 1, Book XII., containing 63 verses, consists of praise and prayer addressed to Prithivi.

Varuna.—There are frequent reference to this deity, the only one to whom moral qualities are specially assigned. His name means the 'coverer' or 'encompasser'; originally the visible starry heavens.

In later times he was connected with the terrestrial ocean and the waters of the earth, and regarded as their presiding deity.

Max Müller says: "This god is one of the most interesting creations of the Hindu mind, because though we can still perceive the physical background from which he rises, the vast, starry brilliant expanse above, his features more than those of any of the Vedic gods, have become completely transfigured, and he stands before us a god who watches over the world, punishes the evil-doer, and ever forgives the sin of those who implore his pardon."*

Varuna is especially the moral governor of the world; "viewing men's righteous and unrighteous dealing, seizing evil-doers in his noose and punishing them."

Hymn 16, Book IV. celebrates the omnipresence and omniscience of Varuna; but concludes with an imprecation on an enemy. The last verse may be an addition. *Both the oceans*, denote the ocean of air, and the ocean of water.

1 The mighty Ruler of these worlds beholds as though from close at hand
The man who thinks he acts by stealth; all this the Gods perceive and know.

2 If a man stands or walks or moves in secret, goes to his lying-down or his uprising,
What two men whisper as they sit together, King Varuna knows: he as the third is present.

3 This earth, too, is King Varuna's possession, and the high heaven whose ends are far asunder.
The loins of Varuna are both the oceans, and this small drop of water, too, contains him.

* *India, What can it Teach us?* p. 195.

4 If one should flee afar beyond the heaven, King Varuna would still be round about him.
Proceeding hither from the sky his envoys look, thousand-eyed, over the earth beneath them.
5 All this the royal Varuna beholdeth, all between heaven and earth and all beyond them.
The twinklings of men's eyelids hath he counted. As one who plays throws dice he settles all things.
6 Those fatal snares of thine which stand extended, threefold, O Varuna, seven by seven,
May they all catch the man who tells a falsehood, and pass unharmed the man whose words are truthful.
7 Varuna, snare him with a hundred nooses! Man's watcher! let not him who lies escape thee.
There let the villain sit with hanging belly and bandaged like a cask whose hoops are broken.
8 Varuna sends, and drives away, diseases: Varuna is both native and a stranger,
Varuna is celestial and is human.
9 I bind and hold thee fast with all these nooses, thou son of such a man and such a mother.
All these do I assign thee as thy portion.

Savitar.—This god takes an important place in the Atharva-Veda. His title is derived from *su*, to beget. He is regarded as a generative power, sometimes identified with, sometimes distinguished from Súrya. He is especially the morning sun whose light drives away witches and evil spirits. The celebrated Gáyatrí is addressed to Savitar. It is supposed to exert magical powers.

Tat Savitur vareṇyam bhargo devasya dhímahi |
dhiyo yo nah prachodayát | R. V. iii. 62, 10.

It has been variously translated. Griffith renders it thus:

"May we attain that excellent glory of Savitar the god:
So may he stimulate our prayers."

Wilson says that it was "in its original use, a simple invocation of the sun to shed a benignant influence upon the customary offices of worship." The Skanda Purana extols it as "Vishnu, Brahma, Siva, and the Three Vedas."

In Hymn 4, Book XIII., quoted below, Savitar is praised as comprehending in himself all other divinities, as the only divinity.

1 Down looking on the ridge of sky, Savitar goes to highest heaven.
2 To misty cloud filled with his rays Mahendra goes encompassed round.
3 Creator and Ordainer, he is Váyu, he is lifted cloud.
4 Rudra and Mahádeva, he is Aryaman and Varuna.
5 Agni is he and Súrya, he is verily Maháyama.
11 He keepeth watch o'er creatures, all that breatheth and that breatheth not.

12 This conquering might hath entered him. He is the sole, the simple One, the One alone.
18 In him these Deities become simple and One.
32 He was produced from Wind; and Wind derives his origin from him.
33 From Heaven was he produced; and Heaven derives his origin from him.
55 Worship to thee whom all behold! Regard me, thou whom all regard,
56 With food, and fame, and vigour, with the splendour of a Brahman's rank.

Soma.—The references to Soma as the god, the juice of the plant, and the moon, are very numerous. The plant was formerly supposed to be a milky climbing plant (*Asclepias acida*) ; it is now identified with a species of Ephedra, which in the Harirud valley is said to bear the name of *hum, huma, and yahma.**

PAVAMANA denotes the deified Soma as it passes through the purifying filter.

Soma is the god of plants, they being supposed to thrive especially under the influence of the moon.

In Hymn 96, Book VI. the many plants that Soma rules as King, are asked to deliver the suppliants from grief and woe. He himself is asked to cleanse them from sin.

1 The many plants of hundred shapes and forms that Soma, rules as King,
Commanded by Brihaspati, deliver us from grief and woe!
2 Let them release me from the curse and from the noose of Varuna,
Free me from Yama's fetter, and from every sin against the gods!
3 From every fault in look, in word, or spirit that we, awake or sleeping, have committed,
May Soma, with his godlike nature, cleanse us.

Ushas.—The Dawn, the morning light personified, is several times mentioned. Bhaga, conqueror in the morning, as the early sun overpowers Ushas, called his sister. Ushas is also called the daughter of Prajapati whom he wished to marry, a proceeding which shocked the gods. Rig-Veda X. 61. 5–8. This was understood literally, but Kumarila explained it as only meaning that at sunrise, the sun runs after the dawn. In Hymn 12, Book XIX, quoted below, she is asked for wealth and long life:

Dawn drives away her sister's gloom, and through her excellence makes her retrace her path.
Through her may we gain god-appointed treasure, and with brave sons be glad through hundred winters.

Pushan.—The name is derived from *push*, to nourish. As a god he protects and multiplies cattle and human possessions

* Griffith, Vol. I. p. 252.

generally. As a form of the Sun, he beholds the entire universe. Travellers especially pray to him for protection.

Hymn 9, Book VII. is as follows:

1 Pûshan was born to move on distant pathways, on roads remote from earth, remote from heaven.
To both most lovely places of assembly he travels and returns with perfect knowledge.
2 Pûshan knows all these realms: may he conduct us by ways that are most free from fear and danger.
Giver of blessings, glowing, all heroic, may he the wise and watchful go before us.
3 We are thy praisers here, O Pûshan: never let us be injured under thy protection.
4 From out the distance, far and wide, may Pûshan stretch his right hand forth.
Let him drive back our lost to us, let us return with what is lost.

Vayu.—There are several references to Váyu, the god of Wind, a deity of the middle region of the air. He refreshes the cattle and drives off the flies. He is one of the eight Lokapálas or world-protectors who preside over the eight points of the compass. He is praised as the god of the air which supports life.

Váyu is invoked in several hymns, and Hymn 4, Book VII. is specially addressed to him. Its repetition three times concludes the ceremony of blessing the horses.

With thine eleven teams to aid our wishes, yea, with thy two-and-twenty teams, O Váyu,
With all thy three-and-thirty teams for drawing, here loose these teams, thou who art prompt to listen!

Skambha.—Hymn 7, Book X, is a glorification of the Supreme Deity embodied, under this name, the Pillar or Support of all existence. On him Prajapati set up and established all the worlds. In his body are contained all three-and-thirty deities. He is called "the Unborn," "the highest Brahman"; but he is also identified with Indra.

It is a long hymn containing 44 verses. The following are some quotations.

7 Who out of many, tell me, is that Skambha
On whom Prajápati set up and firmly stablished all the worlds?
8 That universe which Prajápati created, wearing all forms, the highest, midmost, lowest,
How far did Skambha penetrate within it? What portion did he leave unpenetrated?
13 Who out of many, tell me, is that Skambha,
He in whose body are contained all three-and-thirty Deities?
14 Who out of many, tell me, is that Skambha
In whom the Sages earliest born, the Richas, Sáman, Yajus, Earth, and the one highest Sage abide?

15 Who out of many, tell me, is that Skambha
Who comprehendeth, for mankind, both immortality and death,
He who containeth for mankind the gathered waters, as his veins?

20 Who out of many, tell me, is that Skambha
From whom they hewed the Richas off, from whom they chipped the Yajus, he
Whose hairs are Sáma-verses, and his mouth the Atharvángirases?

39 Who out of many, tell me, is that Skambha
To whom the Deities with hands, with feet, and voice, and ear, and eye
Present unmeasured tribute in the measured hall of sacrifice?

The Unknown God.—Hymn 2, Book IV. is taken, with some variations, from Rig-Veda, X. 121. After each verse the question is asked, "What God shall we adore with our oblation?" *Ka*, who, was adopted as the name of a god. "Worship we Ka, the god, with our oblation."

1 Giver of breath, giver of strength and vigour, he whose commandment all the Gods acknowledge,
He who is Lord of this, of man and cattle:—What God shall we adore with our oblation?

2 Who by his grandeur hath become sole ruler of all the moving world that breathes and slumbers,
Whose shade is death, whose lustre makes immortal:—
What God shall we adore with our oblation?

3 To whom both hosts embattled, look with longing, and Heaven and Earth invoke him in their terror;
Whose is this path that measures out the region:—
What God shall we adore with our oblation?

4 Whose is the mighty earth and spacious heaven, and yonder ample firmament between them,
Whose is yon Sun extended in his grandeur:—
What God shall we adore with our oblation?

5 Whose, through his might, are all the Snowy Mountains, and whose, they say is Rasâ in the ocean,
The arms of whom are these celestial quarters:—
What God shall we adore with our oblation?

6 The deathless Waters, born in Law, receiving, protected all the germ in the beginning,—
Waters divine who had the God above them:—
What God shall we adore with our oblation?

7 In the beginning rose Hiranyagarbha, even at his birth sole Lord of all creation.
He fixt and firmly stablished earth and heaven:—
What God shall we adore with our oblation?

8 In the beginning, generating offspring, the Waters brought an embryo into being;
And even as it sprang to life it had a covering of gold.

Purusha.—The subject of Hymn 2, Book X, is "Púrusha," the Primeval Man, or Humanity Personified. In stanzas 16 and 18 quoted below, he is identified with Brahma, the Phenomenal Creator.

1 Who framed the heels of Púrusha? who fashioned the flesh of him? Who formed and fixed his ankles?
Who made the openings and well-moulded fingers? Who gave him foot-soles and a central station?

4 Who and how many were those gods who fastened the chest of Púrusha and neck together?
How many fixed his breasts? Who formed his elbows? How many joined together ribs and shoulders?

16 Through whom did he spread waters out, through whom did he make Day to shine.
Through whom did he enkindle Dawn and give the gift of eventide?

18 Through whom did he bedeck the earth, through whom did he encompass heaven?
Whose might made Púrusha surpass the mountains and created things?

Hymn 6, Book XIX. is taken, with some variations, from Rig-Veda X. 90, known as the Púrusha-Sukta, a pantheistic hymn in which the four castes are mentioned:

1 Purusha hath a thousand arms, a thousand eyes, a thousand feet.
On every side pervading earth he fills a space ten fingers wide.

2 He with three quarters rose to heaven: here reappeared a fourth of him.
Thence he strode forth on every side to all that eats not and that eats.

3 So mighty is his grandeur, yea, greater than this is Purusha.
All creatures are one-fourth of him, three-fourths what dieth not in heaven.

4 Purusha is in truth this All, what hath been and what yet shall be—
Lord, too, of immortality—and what hath grown with somewhat else.

5 When they divided Purusha how many portions did they make?
What was his mouth? What were his arms? What are the names of thighs and feet?

6 The Brahman was his mouth, of both his arms was the Rajanya made.
His waist became the Vaisya, from his feet the Sudra was produced.

7 The Moon was gendered from his mind, and from his eye the Sun had birth.
Indra and Agni from his mouth were born, and Váyu from his breath.

8 Forth from his navel came mid-air; the sky was fashioned from his head,
Earth from his feet, and from his ear the regions. Thus they formed the worlds.
9 In the beginning rose Virâj: Purusha from Virâj was born.
As soon as he was born he spread westward and eastward o'er the earth.
10 When Gods performed the sacrifice with Purusha as their offering.
Spring was the butter, summer was the fuel, autumn was the gift.
11 That sacrifice, first-born Purusha, they hallowed with the sprinkled Rains.
The Deities, the Sâdhyas, all the Vasus sacrificed with him.
12 From it were horses born, from it all creatures with two rows of teeth.
From it were generated kine, from it were goats and sheep produced.
13 From that great general sacrifice Richas and Sâma hymns were born:
Therefrom the metres were produced: the Yajus had its birth from it.
14 From that great general sacrifice the dripping fat was gathered up:
It formed the creatures fleet as wind, and animals both wild and tame.
15 Seven fencing-logs had he, thrice seven layers of fuel were prepared.
When, offering sacrifice, the Gods bound as their victim Purusha.
16 Forth from the head of the high God seven-and-seventy bright beams
Sprang into being, of the King Soma produced from Purusha.

Vishnu.—The references to this god, who afterwards rose to such eminence, are not numerous, and he is chiefly mentioned in connection with other deities. In the Veda he is the Sun, the "Wide-Strider," who traverses the world in three strides, his rising, culmination, and setting. Hymn 26, Book VII. seems the only hymn specially addressed to him, and it is mostly taken from the Rig-Veda I. *Homed in oil,* denotes dwelling in the molten butter used in sacrifice.

1 I will declare the mighty deeds of Vishnu, of him who measured out the earthly regions,
Who propped the highest place of congregation, thrice setting down his footstep, widely striding.
2 Loud boast doth Vishnu make of this achievement, like some wild beast, dread, prowling, mountain-roaming.
May he approach us from the farthest distance.

3 Thou within whose three wide-extended paces all worlds and creatures have their habitation,
Drink oil, thou homed in oil! promote the sacrificer more and more.
4 Through all this world strode Vishnu: thrice his foot he planted and the whole
Was gathered in his footstep's dust.
5 Vishnu the guardian, he whom none deceiveth, made three steps, thenceforth
Establishing these high decrees.
6 Look ye on Vishnu's works, whereby the friend of Indra, close-allied,
Hath let his holy ways be seen.
7 The princes evermore behold that loftiest place where Vishnu is,
Like an extended eye in heaven.
8 From heaven, O Vishnu, or from earth, O Vishnu, or from the great far-spreading air's mid-region,
Fill both thy hands full of abundant treasures, and from the right and left bestow them freely.

Rudra.—Rudra, the Howler, the father of the Rudras, has several references. He is represented in two characters—the Destroyer and the Healer. In several hymns deliverance from his darts are asked, both with reference to men and cattle. On the other hand, in Hymn 27, Book II., he is called "Lord of Healing." In Hymn 90, Book VI., he is asked to cure a man who has been poisoned, and in Hymn 57, Book VI., to cure a wound. Both have been quoted.

Maruts.—There are several references to the Maruts, literally the 'smashers,' the terrible gods of battle, storm, and tempest, and the gracious senders of refreshing rain. In Hymn 1, Book XIII., they are said to form 9 troops of 7 each, and are called the triple-seven. They are named the Rudras, as the sons of Rudra. In Hymn 15, Book IV., and in others they are asked to make the clouds pour down their waters. In Hymn 1, Book III. they are asked, with Indra and Agni, to destroy enemies. Hymn 27, Book IV., is a prayer to them to save from grief and trouble. The following are extracts:

1 I think upon the Maruts: may they bless me, may they assist me to this wealth in battle.
I call them like swift well-trained steeds to help us. May they deliver us from grief and trouble.
5 They who delight in nectar and in fatness, they who bestow upon us health and vigour,
The Maruts who rain mighty with their waters, may they deliver us from grief and trouble.
6 Whether with stormy might the Maruts stablished this all, or Gods with their celestial power,
Ye, kindly Gods, are able to restore it. May they deliver us from grief and trouble.

7 Potent in battles is the Maruts' army, impetuous train, well-known, exceeding mighty.
I, suppliant, praise and oft invoke the Maruts. May they deliver us from grief and trouble.

GODDESSES.—In the Vedas the female deities occupy a very subordinate position compared with later times. A few may be briefly noticed.

Indrani.—This goddess is the wife of Indra. In Hymn 27, Book I., she is asked to guide a traveller. In Hymn 126, Book XX., taken from the Rig-Veda X. 86, she boasts of her charms, &c.

She says to Indra:

6 No dame hath ampler charms than I, or greater wealth of love's delights.

Indra acknowledges this:

8 Dame with the lovely hands and arms, with broad hair-plaits and ample hips.

Sarasvati.—In the Atharva-Veda she is a female divinity of the upper region, guardian of the waters, and bestower of fertility. She is also identified with Vach, the goddess of speech. In the Puranas she is the wife of Brahmá, the patroness of learners.

Hymn 10, Book VII., a prayer to Sarasvatí taken with variations from the Rig-Veda, was used to soothe an infant, probably when teething.

That breast of thine, exhaustless and delightful, good to invoke, beneficent, free-giver,
Wherewith thou feedest all things that are choicest, bring that, Sarasvatí, that we may drain it.

Vak or **Vach.**—The Goddess of Speech has several references. She is speech personified, the word, the first creation and representative of Spirit, and the means of communication between men and gods. Hymn 30, Book IV., taken from Rig-Veda X. 125, is a glorification of Vak. She thus states her claims:

2 I am the Queen, the gatherer-up of treasures, most thoughtful, first of those who merit worship.
The Gods, making me enter many places, in divers spots have set mine habitation.

3 I, verily, myself announce and utter the word that Gods and men alike shall welcome.
I make the man I love exceeding mighty, make him a sage, a Rishi, and a Brahman.

7 On the world's summit I bring forth the Father: my home is in the waters, in the ocean.
Thence I extend o'er all existing creatures, and touch even yonder heaven with my forehead.

Note.—The Father; Dyaus=Zeus, Heaven or Sky produced from Vák, identified with Paramátma, the supreme or universal soul.

Sinivali, "broad-tressed," is the goddess of the day of new moon; also of fecundity and easy birth like the Latin goddess Lucina. In Hymn 25, Book V. she is asked to bless conception. In Hymn 26, Book II. she is asked to guide the cattle home. In Hymn 46, Book VII., quoted below, she is styled "Queen of Men," "Consort of Vishnu," and is asked to bestow children.

1 O broad-tressed Siníválí, thou who art the sister of the Gods,
Accept the offered sacrifice, and, Goddess, grant us progeny.

2 Present the sacrifice to her, to Siníválí, Queen of men,
Beautiful-fingered, lovely-armed, prolific, bearing many a child.

3 Thou who as Queen of men art Indra's equal, a Goddess coming with a thousand tresses.
To thee our sacrifices are performed, O Consort of Vishnu: Goddess, urge thy Lord to bounty!

Other goddesses are simply named; as Agnayí, Asviní, Rodasí, wife of Rudra, and Varunaní in Hymn 49, Book VII.—a prayer to the goddesses for children and booty.

PRAYERS FOR THE PARDON OF SIN.

One of the most deadly errors in the teaching of Swami Vivekananda is his denial of man's sinfulness. In his Chicago address he said:

"'Children of immortal bliss,' what a sweet, what a hopeful name! Allow me to call you, brethren, by that sweet name—heirs of immortal bliss—yea, the Hindu refuses to call you sinners.

"Ye are the children of God, the sharers of immortal bliss, holy and perfect beings. Ye, divinities on earth, sinners? It is a sin to call a man so."

It is only pride and ignorance that make a man deny that he is a sinner. The holiest men are the first to acknowledge it. Some Brahmans daily make this acknowledgment:

Pápo'ham pápakarmáham pápátma pápasambhavah.

"I am sin; I commit sin; my soul is sinful; I am conceived in sin."

If men are "holy and perfect beings," what is the need of bathing in the Ganges or other supposed sacred waters?

The teaching of the Swami is contradicted both by the Rig-Veda and the Atharva-Veda. Some hymns from the latter on this point will be quoted.

The hymn to Varuna (see page 48) acknowledges his omnipresence and omniscience. "If one should flee afar beyond the heaven, King Varuna would still be round about him." "The twinklings of men's eyelids hath he counted."

Sin is not thought to be limited to outward acts. Hymn 96, Book VI. contains the following petition :

3 From every fault in look, in word, in spirit that we, awake or sleeping, have committed,
May Soma, with his godlike nature, cleanse us.

Hymn 45, Book VI., also refers to mental sins and seeks forgiveness :

1 Sin of the Mind, avaunt ! begone ! Why sayest thou what none should say ?
Go hence away, I love thee not. Go to the forests and the trees. My heart is in our homes and cows.
2 Whatever wrong we have committed, sleeping or waking, by ill-wish, dislike, or slander,
All these offences, which deserve displeasure, may Agni take from us and keep them distant.
3 Indra and Brahmanaspati ! whatever foolish deed we plan,
May provident Angirasa preserve us from the sin and woe.

NOTE.—Verses 2 and 3 are taken from Rig-Veda, X. 164.

Prayers for the pardon of sin an addressed to several gods, especially Varuna.

To Varuna. Book VII. 83.

1 Stablished amid the waters is, King Varuna, thy golden home.
Thence let the Sovran who maintains the statutes loose all binding cords.
2 Hence free thou us, King Varuna, from each successive bond and tie.
As we have cried, O Varuna ! have said, The Waters, they are kine, thence set us free, O Varuna.
3 Loosen the bonds, O Varuna, that hold us, loosen the bond above, between, and under.
So before Aditi may we be sinless under thy favouring auspices, Aditya!
4 Varuna, free us from all snares that bind us, Varuna's bonds, the upper and the lower.
Drive from us evil dream, drive off misfortune : then let us pass into the world of virtue.

To the Visvedevas. Book VI. 115.

1 Whatever wrong we wittingly or in our ignorance have done,
Do ye deliver us therefrom, O all ye Gods, of one accord.
2 If I, a sinner, when awake or sleeping have committed sin,
Free me therefrom as from a stake, from present and from future guilt.
3 As one unfastened from a stake, or cleansed by bathing after toil,
As butter which the sieve hath cleaned, so all shall purge me from the sin.

To Plants ruled by Soma. Book VI. 96.

1 The many plants of hundred shapes and forms that Soma rules as King,
Commanded by Brihaspati, deliver us from grief and woe!

2 Let then release me from the curse and from the noose of Varuna,
Free me from Yama's fetter, and from every sin against the Gods.

Note.—The concluding verse has already been quoted, see page 57.

To Agni. Book VII. 106.

Pardon is asked by priests for any error in conducting divine service:

Each thoughtless ill that we have done, O Agni,
All error in our conduct, Játavedas!
Therefrom do thou, O sapient God, preserve us,
May we thy friends, for bliss, have life eternal.

In Hymn 120, Book VI., Agni Gárhapatya, the sacred fire perpetually maintained by a householder, received from his father and transmitted to his son, is asked for pardon:

1 If we have injured Air, or Earth, or Heaven, if we have wronged our mother or our father,
May Agni Gárhapatya here absolve us, and bear us up into the world of virtue.

Absolution for having offended Varuna. Book I. 10.

1 This Lord is the Gods' ruler; for the wishes of Varuna the King must be accomplished.
Therefore, triumphant with the prayer I utter, I rescue this man from the Fierce One's anger.

2 Homage be paid, King Varuna, to thine anger; for thou, dread God, detectest every falsehood.
I send a thousand others forth together: let this thy servant live a hundred autumns.

3 Whatever falsehood thou hast told, much evil spoken with the tongue,
I liberate thee from the noose of Varuna the righteous King.

4 I free thee from Vaisvánara, from the great surging flood of sin.
Call thou thy brothers, Awful One! and pay attention to our prayer.

NOTES.—The hymn is supposed to be spoken by a priest after intercession with Varuna. *I send a thousand others forth:* he interceded only for this man; others might be punished. *The noose:* borne by Varuna to capture the evil-doer. *Vaisvánara* ruling all men,—here Varuna. *Call thy brothers:* the other Adityas, that they may see that this man has been pardoned.

REFERENCES TO A FUTURE STATE.

Little is said directly about a place of punishment, although suffering is frequently acknowledged as the just desert of sin. The Pitris are supposed to avenge evil deeds as well as Varuna. Hymn 1, Book XVIII. says:

> 52 Punish us not for any sin, O Fathers, which we, through human frailty, have committed.

The place of punishment is said to be *below*. Hymn 128, Book XX. says:

> 2 He who defiles a sister, he who willingly would harm a friend,
> The fool who slights his elder, these, they say, must suffer down below.

In Hymn 3, Book X. it is thus described:

> 9 Pass to the region void of light: to deepest darkness let them go.

The references to Svarga, heaven, are more numerous. The belief in transmigration had not yet been developed, and worshippers hoped to join in heaven their departed relations. VI. 120.

> 2 Dyaus, Father, save us from the world of Fathers!
> My world not lost, may I approach my kindred.
> 3 There where our virtuous friends, who left behind them their bodily infirmities, are happy,
> Free from distortion of the limbs and lameness, may we behold, in heaven, our sons and parents.

In Hymn 34, Book IV. heaven is the reward of the Vishtárí sacrifice, consisting chiefly of an oblation of mashed rice and milk. The description given in it of heaven is quoted below:

> 5 Strongest is this, performed, of sacrifices: he hath reached heaven who hath prepared Vishtárí.
> The oval-fruited lotus spreads his fibre: there bloom the nenuphar and water-lilies.
> Abundant with their overflow of sweetness, these streams shall reach thee in the world of Svarga, whole lakes with lotus-blossom shall approach thee.
> 6 Full lakes of butter with their banks of honey, flowing with wine, and milk, and curds, and water—
> Abundant with their overflow of sweetness, these streams shall reach thee in the world of Svarga, whole lakes with lotus-blossom shall approach thee.

NOTE.—A more attractive account of Svarga is given in Rig-Veda, ix. 113.

Sacrifices go to heaven, and are stored up as merit to await the sacrificer on his arrival. The victim sacrificed also goes to heaven: hence the Buddhists advised them to sacrifice their parents to secure their future happiness! Hymn 123, Book VI. is as follows:

> 1 Ye who are present, unto you I offer this treasure brought to us by Játavedas.
> Happily will the sacrificer follow: do ye acknowledge him in highest heaven.
> 2 Do ye acknowledge him in highest heaven: ye know the world here present in assembly.
> In peace will he who sacrifices follow: show him the joy which comes from pious actions.
> 3 Gods are the Fathers, and the Fathers Gods. I am the very man I am.
> 4 I cook, I give, I offer up oblation. From what I gave let me not be disparted.
> 5 O King, take thou thy stand in heaven, there also let that gift be placed.
> Recognize, King, the gift which we have given, and be gracious, God!

In Hymn 34, Book II. the slaughtered animal is thus addressed:

> 5 Go to the sky. Stay there with all thy members.
> By paths which Gods have travelled go to Svarga.

Although, in the great majority of cases, heaven is said to be the result of sacrifice, some other actions have the same reward. Hymn 6, Book IX. says: "9 With the couch that the men bring (for a guest), he wins for himself the world of Svarga," "23 Now these guests, as priests beloved or not beloved, bring one to the world of Svarga."

REVIEW.

The Atharva, or Fourth, Veda, has been described in detail, and many illustrative quotations have been given.

The book may be viewed under several aspects. It presents a vivid picture of life in the times when it was composed. We can trace the history of the people who then lived from their birth as infants until, at the funeral pile, their spirits are addressed:

> Go forth, go forth upon the homeward pathways whither our sires of old have gone before us.

On many points we can sympathise with them. They had their daily occupations, their bodily ailments, their hopes and fears, their joys and sorrows, just like ourselves. The human race is substantially the same. "He fashioneth their hearts alike."

Compared with the times of the Rig-Veda, the Aryans had advanced farther into India, occupying the plains of the Ganges and Jumna. Struggles with the Dasyus have not such a prominent place. Most of the hymns addressed to the soma-drinking Indra are taken from the Rig-Veda, and are later additions. A large proportion of the hymns have reference to ordinary daily life.

The hymns about women show that, as in the times of the Rig-Veda, the present system of infant marriage did not prevail. Marriages were not simply arranged by parents; brides were grown up, and expected to manage their households, instead of being placed under mothers-in-law (see page 43.)

Among the points of difference the following may be noticed:

1. **The Development of Caste.**—In the Rig-Veda the four castes are only once mentioned in a hymn of comparatively recent origin. As represented in the Atharva-Veda, the system had made great progress. The four castes are repeatedly mentioned. The Brahmans had attained a high position. The sin and evil consequences of injuring them in any way are shown in the strongest terms.

2. **Increased belief in Magic and Witchcraft.**—It is true that in the Rig-Veda, there are some charms and a reference to sorceresses; but in the Atharva-Veda they are much more numerous. Madame Ragozin's opinion has been quoted, that the change was brought about by contact with the aborigines. Throughout the whole of Eastern Asia, demonolatry was the original superstition. Nine classes of malignant spirits are enumerated at page 25.

Belief in charms is characteristic of a low state of civilization. The negroes of West Africa have great faith in them. Anything may be employed as a charm. It may be a bit of wood, a stone, a piece of rag, a feather, a bone, hair, earth from a grave, &c. They are generally tied up in a piece of cloth or leather, and worn around the neck, arms, waist, or legs. A baby has one tied round him soon after he is born, and as he grows in years he often adds charm after charm, till his body is covered with them.

The Burmese can never lose their charms, for there are few who have not charms of some kind tattooed on the arms, back, chest, or even on the top of the head, which is shaved for the purpose. These figures are of all kinds—lizards, birds, mystic words and squares, rings, images of Buddha, and sometimes merely a few scattered dots. The colouring matter is almost always red.

Some of these tattooed charms are supposed to prevent a person from feeling pain when beaten, others guard against danger from snake-bite, musket-shots, drowning, the spells of wizards, and evil spirits. It does not matter to the Burmese although persons having tattooed charms are shot or drowned. Their belief in their efficacy is practically ineradicable.

The principal objects employed in the charms mentioned in the Atharva-Veda were plants, the wood of certain trees, metals; &c.

All these are worthless; their powers are imaginary.

Belief in witchcraft is another characteristic of savages.

Among the Kafirs of South Africa, if a person gets sick, it is believed that some enemy has bewitched him, and a witch-doctor is employed to "smell out" the man who has caused the injury. Until this is done, no one expects him to get better. No medicine is given; they have only charms. Once a chief got a bad cold. A witch-doctor said it was caused by a poor old man, who was forthwith killed.

The prevalence of witchcraft among the aboriginal tribes of India has already been noticed (p. 13).

Uselessness of Charms.—This is shown in three ways:

1. Mere words have no power. What is considered the strongest charm cannot hurt even a fly. People may trample charms under foot, cut them in pieces, throw them into the fire. If they cannot protect themselves, much less can they protect those who wear them.

2. The demons of which the people of India stand so much in dread have no existence. They are like the imaginary goblins by which some ignorant parents try to frighten their children. There are no such beings as Sitala Devi, Mari Amman, &c.

3. The nations of the world that suffer least from sickness and live longest, who are the most prosperous, never use charms, while they abound among savage tribes.

The belief in witchcraft is equally groundless.

THE GODS OF THE ATHARVA-VEDA.

The deities mentioned are much the same as those in the Rig-Veda. Agni and Indra are the two most prominent. The other gods and goddesses have been described.

Some good features of the hymns may first be noticed.

1. **Recognition of God's Omniscience and Omnipresence.**—These are stated with great force and beauty in the hymn to Varuna already quoted (pp. 47, 48).

2. **A Sense of Sin.**—As already mentioned, the feeling is not confined to outward acts. Faults in look or spirit, committed asleep or awake, are acknowledged.

3. **Prayer and Praise.**—It is true that nearly all the petitions refer merely to temporal benefits. The 'Morning Prayer' of Vasishtha, one of the greatest of the Vedic Rishis, is as follows:

1 Agni at dawn, and Indra we invoke at dawn, and Varuna, and
Mitra, and the Asvins twain:
Bhaga at dawn, Pûshan, and Brahmanaspati, Soma at dawn,
and Rudra we invoke at dawn.

2 We call strong Bhaga, conqueror in the morning, the son of
Aditi, the great Disposer,
Whom each who deems himself poor, strong and mighty, a king,
addresses thus, Grant thou my portion!

3. Bhaga, our guide, Bhaga whose gifts are faithful, favour this hymn, and give us wealth, O Bhaga.
Bhaga, augment our store of kine and horses, Bhaga, may we be rich in men and heroes.

4 So may felicity be ours at present, and when the Sun advances, and at noontide;
And may we still, O Bounteous One, at sunset be happy in the Gods' protecting favour.

5 May Bhaga verily be bliss-bestower, and through him, Gods! may happiness attend us.
As such with all my might I call and call thee: as such be thou our leader here, O Bhaga.

6 To this our sacrifice may the Dawns incline them, and come to the pure place like Dadhikrávan.
As strong steeds draw a chariot may they bring me hitherward Bhaga who discovers treasure.

7 May the kind Mornings dawn on us for ever with wealth of kine, of horses, and of heroes.
Streaming with all abundance, pouring fatness. Do ye preserve us evermore with blessings!

The above hymn, Book III. 16 of the Atharva-Veda, is taken with slight variations from Book VII. 41, of the Rig-Veda. *Bhaga* means blessed, adorable. He is here called "conqueror in the morning", as the early Sun overpowering Ushas, the Dawn.

It will be observed that there is not a single petition for spiritual blessings. A hymn has been quoted in which deliverance is asked from a debt contracted without intention of repayment; in another the request is for success in gambling. Still, on the whole, the feeling is commendable. In Hymn 19, Book I., the acknowledgment is made, "Our choicest, closest armour is prayer."

THE ATHARVA-VEDA NOT A DIVINE REVELATION.

The common belief of the Hindus is that the Vedas are entirely of divine origin, breathed out by Brahma after each destruction of the universe. Of this there is not the slightest proof, and an examination of the Atharva-Veda shows that the belief is untenable.

1. The Polytheism of the Vedas disproves their divine origin.—Polytheism is a belief in *many* gods; Monotheism, declares that there is only *one* God. The former is held only by uncivilised or half-civilised nations; the latter is the creed of enlightened people throughout the world.

The simple-minded Aryans deified the common objects of nature. Many of the Vedic hymns are invocations of the fire, the water, the sky, the sun, the moon, &c. Fire, so useful to man, was worshipped under the name of Agni, and became one of the most prominent deities. He was second only to the Rain-god, called Indra, with his thunderbolts, He smote the clouds, and compelled them to give up their watery treasures. A deity so armed would be able to render assistance in battle. Hence he was invoked in struggles with the Dasyus, the aborigines. As soldiers sometimes take strong drink before fighting to give them courage, so Indra was supposed to quaff, like a thirsty stag, draughts of the intoxicating soma juice. The sun, also, took an important place. He was worshipped as Mitra, Súrya, and Savitri. Under the last name he is still invoked in the Gáyatré, considered the most sacred prayer of the Vedas. Vishnu, the 'wide-strider,' was originally a sun-god. The dawn before sunrise was regarded as a goddess. The wind in its gentler aspect was worshipped as Váyu; in storms it was the Maruts or 'smashers.' So with other deities.

It is true that in one or two passages in the Vedas the gods are spoken of as one under different names; but there is overwhelming evidence that the religion of the Vedas is polytheistic. Whitney says:

> "The great mass of Vedic hymns are absorbed in the praise and worship of the multifarious deities of the proper Vedic pantheon, and ignore all conception of a unity, of which these are to be accounted the varying manifestations."*

The assertion that the Hindu gods are the same, though worshipped under different names, is only an excuse for the folly of polytheism put forward by those who are somewhat more intelligent than the masses. Rammohun Roy says: "The Hindus firmly believe in the real existence of innumerable gods and goddesses who possess in their own departments full and independent powers, and to propitiate them, and not the true God, are temples erected and ceremonies performed."

The one true God would not give a false revelation of Himself. The polytheism of the Vedas shows that they did not proceed from Him.

In course of time the Vedic gods changed their character, and were superseded by others. More than 2,000 years ago, Aristotle, a famous Greek philosopher, said, "Men create the gods after their own image, not only with regard to their form, but also with regard to their manner of life." In Vedic times Indra is the soma-drinking martial god who recovers the celestial cows from the fort of Pani, and helps the Aryans in their wars against the aborigines. When the Aryans had overcome their enemies and were settled in India, Indra, as described in the Puranas, "is a gorgeous king of a luxurious and somewhat voluptuous court, where dance and music occupy most of his time." The gods of the

* *Oriental Studies*, &c. p. 94.

Puranas are Hindu Rajas, with their tastes and surroundings, but possessed of superhuman powers.

Cicero, a celebrated Roman, says of his countrymen and the Greeks, "Instead of the transfer to man of that which is divine, they transferred human sins to their gods and experienced again the necessary action."

Any book attributing evil passions to God shows that it was not inspired by Him, but proceeded from the imagination of an evil heart. Brahma is regarded as the Creator, but in the sacred books of the Hindus themselves he is charged with lying, drunkenness, and lust: his conduct was considered so vile, that he was deprived of all worship. Vishnu and Siva are considered the greatest of the gods; but the story of Mohini alone makes one regard their whole history as a wicked invention. The same remark applies to Krishna as described in the Bhagavata Purana. The conduct of the Vallabhachâris shows its pernicious influence.

But educated Hindus now generally admit that the tales in the Puranas are fictions; they adopt as their ideal the Krishna of the Bhagavad Gita, and claim him as Supreme. For a full consideration of his character the reader is referred to the treatise mentioned below.*

It is fully admitted that the Krishna of the Bhagavad Gita stands on a far higher level than the Krishna of the Puranas. The poem is exquisitely composed, and expresses some noble sentiments. Nevertheless, an examination of it shows that it was written by a Vaishnava Brahman, who had the ordinary Hindu polytheistic and pantheistic ideas, who sought to uphold caste and the privileges of his order, while he endeavoured to harmonise some doctrines of Hindu philosophy, and give prominence to Krishna *bhakti*. A blasphemous claim is made that "the Deity" spoke the words which he wrote, and the book was foisted into the Mahâbhârata to get the support of its authority.

The Krishna of the Bhagavad Gita, like the Krishna of the Bhagavata Purana, had no existence. His worship and that of the other Hindu gods is not merely useless but sinful, for it is giving them the honour due to the one true God, the Creator and Preserver of the Universe.

2. **The belief in Magic and Witchcraft proves that the Atharva-Veda is not a Divine revelation.**—It has already been shown that such superstitions are characteristic of rude tribes. The Atharva-Veda has been called the "Cursing Veda" from its many charms, supposed to cause the destruction of enemies. Bloomfield says that the "most salient teaching of the Atharva-

---

* *The Bhagavad Gita*, with an English Translation, Explanatory Notes, and an Examination of its Doctrines. 8vo. 108 pp. 4 As. Post-free, 5 As. Sold by Mr. A. T. Scott, Tract Depôt, Madras.

Veda is sorcery," (p. 7.) All this shows that the Veda did not proceed from God, but is the production of men in a rude state of civilization.

Other Sacred Books of the Hindus.—The Vedas were followed by the BRAHMANAS, the Brahmanas by the UPANISHADS, the foundation of the Vedánta Philosophy. The BHAGAVAD GITA tried to combine philosophical systems, in order to remove some of the objections to which they were liable. The PURANAS are still more modern, each written in praise of some particular deity.

Full accounts of these different works, with English translations in whole or in part, are given in the Series entitled THE SACRED BOOKS OF THE EAST DESCRIBED AND EXAMINED, a list of which is appended.

THE TRUE VEDA.

The Hindu Śastras describe the earth as consisting of a vast central mountain, called Meru, surrounded by seven continents and seven seas. It does not follow because this account of the earth is wrong, that there is no true Geography. In like manner, although the four Vedas of the Hindus are not true revelations, such a revelation may exist. The most enlightened nations of the world believe that this true revelation to be found in the BIBLE, of which a short account will now be given.

Although the Bible is often bound in a single volume, it consists of 66 different books, written at widely different periods in the history of the world. God, at "sundry times and in divers manners" made known His will to men. The Bible is the history of the Divine education of the human race, from its childhood to its manhood. The different books were given as they were needed: step by step, man was led upwards in moral and religious progress.

The first sentence of the Bible contains a great truth, never discovered by the wisdom of man: "In the beginning God created the heavens and the earth." To *create* is to *make out of nothing*. Hindus think that as a man cannot do this, neither can God. They imagine therefore that the universe was formed out of a pre-existing material, called *prakriti*. The Bible teaches that God, by His almighty power, called the world into existence, and that it was gradually made fit for the abode of man.

Hinduism asserts that souls are as eternal as Brahma himself. The Bible teaches that we were made by God. He is our Father by creation. "Have we not all one Father? Hath not one God created us?" Christianity teaches us to address God as our "Father in heaven." It is true that we have been disobedient, rebellious children, but we are earnestly invited to return, asking forgiveness.

The ancestors of Europeans and Aryan Hindus once worshipped the same God under the same name, *Dyaush-Pitar*, Heaven-Father. Max Müller beautifully says:

"Thousands of years have passed away since the Aryan nations separated to travel to the North and the South, the West and the East: they have each formed their languages, they have each founded empires and philosophies, they have each built temples and razed them to the ground; they have all grown older, and it may be wiser and better; but when they search for a name for that which is most exalted and yet most dear to every one of us, when they wish to express both awe and love, the infinite and the finite, they can but do what their old fathers did when gazing up to the eternal sky, and feeling the presence of a Being as far as far and as near as near can be; they can but combine the self-same words and utter once more the primeval Aryan prayer, Heaven-Father, in that form which will endure for ever, 'Our Father, which art in heaven.'"

But the Bible tells us that although God is our Father in heaven, we have been ungrateful, disobedient children. God says, by one of His prophets: "Hear, O heavens, and give ear, O earth: for the Lord hath spoken, I have nourished and brought up children, and they have rebelled against me. The ox knoweth its owner and the ass his master's crib: but Israel doth not know, my people doth not consider."

We may be compared to children who have left their father's house to live among wicked companions. The Bible says that "there is not a just man upon earth that doeth good, and sinneth not;" "all have sinned and come short of the glory of God." We sin in thought as well as in word and deed. The best men have the deepest sense of their own sinfulness.

"The wages of sin is death." The whole human race is liable to this penalty. God, in His great love, devised a plan by which we may be saved from the punishment and power of sin.

All through the history of the world there has been the hope of one who would deliver it from the evil which oppresses it. The generations of man, weak and helpless in themselves, have ever more been looking after ONE in whom they may find all they look for vainly in themselves and in those around them.

The Hindu ideas of incarnation are well-known. Krishna says in the Bhagavad Gita: "Whensoever religion fades and irreligion prevails, then I produce myself." The expectation is general that at the close of the Kali Yug, the Kalki *avatára* will come, when Vishnu, on a white horse, will destroy the wicked, and restore the earth to its original purity. These ideas, though defective, recognise the hope of God descending to the level of the fallen creature and becoming man to lighten the burden of pain and misery under which the universe is groaning.

The Bible teaches that God became incarnate as Jesus Christ for our redemption. He perfectly fulfilled the laws which we had broken, and by His death on the cross He made an atonement for sin. Salvation is now freely offered to all who accept Him truly as their Saviour, and strive to follow His example.

A general account of Christianity is given in the two little books mentioned below:

Short Papers for Seekers after Truth. 12mo. 104 pp. 1 An.

Elements of Christian Truth. 12mo. 71 pp. 1½ An. A series of lectures by the Rev. Dr. Murray Mitchell.

A full account of the wonderful history of the Lord Jesus Christ is given in the New Testament. A Hindu had best begin with the *Gospel of Luke,* which was first written for a convert. A copy of it may be obtained for half an anna at any Bible Depôt. There is a sequel to the Gospel of Luke, by the same author, called *The Acts of the Apostles,* describing the early history of the Christian Church.

To assist in the study of these two books of Scripture, a little work, *The Beginnings of Christianity,* has been published. Besides an Introduction to the two books, it contains two coloured Maps, and an explanatory Vocabulary of words presenting any difficulty. Price 1½ An. Post-free, 2 As.

The *New Testament* may form the next study. English editions may be obtained at prices varying from 1 to 4 As. An introduction to its study, called *The Founder of Christianity,* intended specially for Indian students, is sold at 4 As. post-free. The vernacular edition of the Scriptures would be helpful to many in understanding their meaning. The complete Bible may afterwards be studied, and even during the whole course portions of it may be read, especially the Psalms.

Evidences of Christianity.—There is an excellent manual on this subject by the Rev. Dr. Murray Mitchell, *Letters to Indian Youth on the Evidences of Christianity.*—12mo., 280 pp., price 6 As. post-free.

Prayer for Light.—One of the greatest helps to arrive at religious truth is to seek it earnestly from our Father in heaven. The following short prayer may be offered:

"O all-wise, all-merciful God and Father, pour the bright beams of Thy light into my soul, and guide me into Thy eternal truth."

The following longer prayer has been attributed to Augustine, one of the greatest early Christian writers:

"O Lord, who art the Light, the Way, the Truth, the Life; in whom there is no darkness, error, vanity, nor death; the Light, without which there is darkness; the Way, without which there is wandering; the truth, without which there is error; the Life, without which there is death; say, lord, 'Let there be light,' and I shall see light and eschew darkness; I shall see the way and avoid wandering; I shall see the truth and shun error; I shall see life and escape death. Illuminate, O illuminate my blind soul, which sitteth in darkness and the shadow of death; and direct my feet in the way of peace."

CATALOGUE

OF

GENERAL LITERATURE.

ENGLISH.

Descriptions of Countries and Peoples.

PICTORIAL TOUR ROUND INDIA. Imperial 8vo. 116 pp. 6 As. Post-free, 7½ As.

An imaginary tour round India, with visits to Nepal and Cashmere, describing the principal cities and other objects of interest. With 97 woodcuts illustrative of the Himalayas, Calcutta, Benares, Agra, Delhi, Bombay, Madras, &c.

THE PRINCIPAL NATIONS OF INDIA. 8vo. 160 pp. 4 As. Post-free, 5 As.

An account of 42 Nations and Tribes of India, with specimens of some of their languages, and 55 illustrations.

THE NATIVE STATES OF INDIA AND THEIR PRINCES; WITH NOTICES OF SOME IMPORTANT ZEMINDARIS. 4to. 100 pp. 5 As. Post-free, 6 As.

157 States are described, and 32 portraits are given. The little book will help to enable Indians to understand the vast extent of their country, and what is being done for its improvement.

KASI, OR BENARES, the Holy City of the Hindus. Imperial 8vo. 44 pp. 3 As. Post-free, 4 As.

An account of the city; its Sanskrit schools, ghats, temples, and pilgrimages; with 23 illustrations.

THE GREAT TEMPLES OF INDIA, CEYLON, AND BURMA. Imperial 8vo. 104 pp. with 60 illustrations. 6 As. Post-free, 7½ As.

There are pictures and descriptions of some of the most celebrated Hindu, Sikh, Jain, and Buddhist temples; as Puri, Budh-Gaya, Benares, Hurdwar, Gangotri, Ellora, Elephanta, Amritsar, Gwalior, Tanjore, Srirangam, Kandy, Prome and Mandalay.

BURMA AND THE BURMESE. 4to. 54 pp. 2½ As. Post-free, 3 As.

A description of the manners and customs of the Burmese; an account of their government, religion, and history, with illustrative woodcuts, and portraits of King Theebaw and his Queen.

LANKA AND ITS PEOPLE; or, A DESCRIPTION OF CEYLON. 4to. 72 pp. 3 As. Post-free, 3½ As.

The account of Lanka given in the Ramayana is first mentioned. Its history, and present condition are then described, with numerous illustrative woodcuts.

TIBET: THE HIGHEST COUNTRY IN THE WORLD. 4to. 62 pp. 2½ As.

An account of the country, its productions, the curious customs of the people, their religion, and supposed living incarnations; with numerous illustrations.

PICTURES OF CHINA AND ITS PEOPLE. 4to. 56 pp. 2½ As. Post-free, 3 As.

Extent, History; Manners and Customs of the People; Schools, Examinations; Industries; Travelling; Language and Literature; Government; Religious; India and China compared; with 64 Illustrations.

JAPAN: THE LAND OF THE RISING SUN. 4to. 68 pp. 2½ As. Post-free, 3 As.

With 49 Illustrations. An interesting description of this beautiful country, and an account of the remarkable changes which have taken place in it.

PICTORIAL TOUR ROUND BIBLE LANDS. Imperial 8vo. 100 pp. 6 As. Post-free, 7½ As.

The principal countries mentioned in the Bible and in ancient history are described; as Palestine, Syria, Baylon, Asia Minor, Greece and Italy; with 104 Illustrations.

ARABIA, AND ITS PROPHET. 4to. 64 pp. 2½ As. Post-free, 3 As.

An account of the Arabs; with descriptions of Jeddah, Mecca, Medina; the History of Muhammad and the early Caliphs; the Koran, Muslim Doctrines, Sects, Prayers, Pilgrimage, &c.; with numerous illustrations.

PICTURES OF RUSSIA AND ITS PEOPLES. Imperial 8vo. 83 pp. 5 As. Post-free, 6 As.

A description both of European and Asiatic Russia, including an account of the different races by which they are peopled, their manners and customs, the Government, &c.; with 89 illustrations and maps.

EGYPT: THE LAND OF THE PYRAMIDS. Imperial 8vo. 80 pp. 5 As. Post-free, 6 As.

A description of this interesting country, one of the oldest seats of civilization in the world; its ancient religion, its famous temples and other buildings; the manners and customs of the people, etc.; with numerous illustrations.

THE LAND OF SNOWS: with an account of Missions to Greenland. 4to. 56 pp. 2½ As. Post-free, 3 As.

A description of Greenland, so different from India; giving an account of its people, and the efforts to elevate them; with numerous illustrations.

THE OVERLAND JOURNEY TO ENGLAND. 4to. 72 pp. 3 As.

A description of the principal places passed, with some account of the expense, and directions on arrival in England: copiously illustrated.

PICTORIAL TOUR ROUND ENGLAND, SCOTLAND, AND IRELAND. Imperial 8vo. 114 pp. 6 As. Post-free, 7½ As.

Descriptions of the chief places of interest; Public Schools and Universities; Coal Mines and Manufactures; the British Government; Home Life; England an example and warning to India. With 104 woodcuts, and coloured engraving of the Queen-Empress.

ITALY: ANCIENT AND MODERN. Imperial 8vo. 80 pp. 5 As. Post-free, 6 As.

Remarkable events in the history of the country are described; accounts are given of Rome, Vesuvius, the Buried Cities, and other places of interest; with numerous illustrations.

PICTURES OF WOMEN IN MANY LANDS. Imperial 8vo. 112 pp. 6 As. Post-free, 7½ As.

Descriptions of women, beginning with the most degraded nations of the world, and gradually ascending to the most enlightened; with suggestions, from the review, for Indian women; with 172 illustrations.

Biographies.

STATESMEN OF RECENT TIMES. 8vo. 192 pp. 8 As. Post-free, 9½ As.

Accounts are given of the leading Statesmen in the great countries of the world; as Gladstone, Salisbury, Bismarck, and others. Special notice is taken of those interested in India. In all 182 are mentioned, with 122 portraits.

THE GOVERNORS-GENERAL OF INDIA, First Series. By Henry Morris, M. C. S. (retired) 8vo. 145 pp. 4 As. Post-free, 5 As.

Contains sketches of the lives of Warren Hastings, Lord Cornwallis, Sir John Shore, Marquis Wellesley, the Earl of Minto, and the Marquis of Hastings, with portraits. Interesting personal details are given, such as are not usually found in histories.

THE GOVERNORS-GENERAL OF INDIA, Second Series. By the same author, 8vo. 175 pp. 4 As. Post-free, 5 As.

Includes sketches of Lord Amherst, Lord William Bentinck, Lord Auckland, Lord Ellenborough, Lord Hardinge, and the Marquis of Dalhousie.

The two Series, half bound in cloth, gilt title, 12 As.

SKETCHES OF INDIAN CHRISTIANS; WITH AN INTRODUCTION BY S. SATTHIANADHAN, M.A. 8vo. 268 pp. half cloth with gilt title, 10 As. Post-free, 11½ As.

An account of 42 Indian Protestant Christians; Tamil, Telugu, Canarese, Malayalam, Bengali, Hindustani, Panjabi, Afghan, Gujarati, Marathi, Parsi, and Karen; with several portraits.

ANGLO-INDIAN WORTHIES. By Henry Morris, MADRAS C. S. (Retired.) 8vo. 160 pp. 4 As. Post-free, 5 As. Full cloth; gilt title, 8 As.

Lives of Sir Thomas Munro, Sir John Malcolm, Lord Metcalfe, Mountstuart Elphinstone, James Thomason, Sir Henry Lawrence, Sir James Outram, Sir Donald Macleod, and Sir Bartle Frere, with portraits.

EMINENT FRIENDS OF MAN; or LIVES OF DISTINGUISHED PHILANTHROPISTS. 8vo. 158 pp. 4 As. Post-free, 5 As. Full cloth, gilt title, 10 As.

Sketches of Howard, Oberlin, Granville Sharp, Clarkson, Wilberforce, Buxton, Pounds, Davies of Devauden, George Moore, Montefiore, Livesey, the Earl of Shaftesbury, and others; with remarks on what might be done in India.

SOME NOTED INDIANS OF MODERN TIMES. 8vo. 164 pp. 4 As. Post-free, 5 As.

Sketches of Indian Religious and Social Reformers, Philanthropists, Scholars Statesmen, Judges, Journalists, and others; with several portraits.

MARTIN LUTHER, THE GREAT EUROPEAN REFORMER. 8vo. 109 pp. 2½ As. Post-free, 3 As.

The state of religion in Europe in the time of Luther is described; a full account is given of his undaunted efforts to bring about a reformation; the greater need of a similar change in India is shown, and Luther is held up as an example. 15 illustrations.

BABA PADMANJI. An Autobiography. 8vo. 108 pp. 2½ As. Post-free, 3 As.

An interesting account by himself of this popular Marathi author, describing his conversion from Hinduism to Christianity.

PICTURE STORIES OF NOBLE WOMEN. 4to. 50 pp. 2½ As. Post-free, 3 As.

Accounts of Cornelia, Agrippina, Padmani of Chittore, Lady Jane Grey, Ahaliya Bai, Mrs. Fry, Princess Alice, Miss Carpenter, Maharani Surnomayi, Pandita Ramabai, Miss Nightingale, and Lady Dufferin.

THE QUEEN-EMPRESS OF INDIA AND HER FAMILY. 43 pp. 3 As. Post-free, 3½ As.

Her early life; marriage; widowhood; children; progress in India during her reign; traits of character and lessons from her life. With 27 illustrations, and coloured portrait of the Empress.

SIR HERBERT EDWARDES. By Henry Morris. 8vo. 20 pp. ½ Anna.

He is described as the hero of Multan; the peacemaker among wild Afghan tribes; the true friend of India; the earnest Christian.

CHARLES GRANT: The Christian Director of the East India Company. By Henry Morris. 8vo. 48 pp. 1 Anna.

Mr. Grant was an esteemed Indian Civilian, who, after his retirement, became a Director and Chairman for a time of the East India Company. Some very important beneficial changes introduced by him are described. With a portrait.

JOHN CHRYSOSTOM: "THE GOLDEN-MOUTHED." 4to. 52 pp. 2 As.

An account of the most eloquent Christian preacher in ancient times; with a description of the age in which he lived, and the sufferings he endured. Illustrated by engravings.

SOCIAL REFORM.

ON DECISION OF CHARACTER AND MORAL COURAGE. 8vo. 56 pp. 1½ As. Post-free, 2 As.

A reprint of Foster's Celebrated Essay, with some remarks on its application to India.

SANITARY REFORM IN INDIA. 55 pp. 2 As. Post-free, 2½ As.

How lakhs of Lives may be saved every year, and crores of cases of Sickness prevented; Precautions against Fever, Cholera, Diabetes, &c.

IS INDIA BECOMING POORER OR RICHER? WITH REMEDIES FOR THE EXISTING POVERTY. 8vo. 82 pp. 2½ As. Post-free, 3 As.

The prevailing idea with regard to the increasing poverty of India shown to be incorrect, and the true means of promoting its wealth explained.

DEBT AND THE RIGHT USE OF MONEY. 8vo. 32 pp. 1 Anna.

Prevalence of Debt in India; its Causes; Evils; how to get out of it; with Franklin's Way to Wealth, &c.

PURITY REFORM. 8vo. 32 pp. 1 Anna.

The great need of this reform shown, and the means for its promotion.

TEMPERANCE REFORM IN INDIA. 8vo. 40 pp. 1½ As. Post-free, 2 As.

Intoxicating liquors in Ancient India; Intemperance in England; Temperance Reform in the West; spread of Intemperance in India; Temperance Reform in India; how to promote Temperance Reform; with Portraits of Livesey, Father Mathew, Sir Wilfred Lawson, Dean Farrar, Messrs. Samuel Smith and Caine.

CASTE. 8vo. 66 pp. 2 As. Post-free, 2½ As.

Supposed and real origin of Caste; Laws of Caste according to Manu; its Effects; Duty with regard to it.

THE WOMEN OF INDIA AND WHAT CAN BE DONE FOR THEM. 8vo. 158 pp. 4 As. Post-free, 5½ As.

Women in Hindu literature; Female Education; Marriage Customs; Widow Marriage; means to be adopted to raise the position of Women.

THE ABOVE COMPLETE IN ONE VOLUME, 1 Rupee Net. Postage, 2½ As.

PRIZE ESSAY ON THE PROMOTION OF INDIAN DOMESTIC REFORM. 8vo. 144 pp. 4 As. Post-free, 5 As.

The prize was gained by Ganpat Lakshman, of Bombay, in 1841. His Essay was published with a Prefatory Note by the Rev. Dr. John Wilson, in which it is highly commended as giving a graphic and correct picture of Hindu family life.

RELIGIOUS REFORM.

A RATIONAL REFUTATION OF THE HINDU PHILOSOPHICAL SYSTEMS. 2nd Edition. 8vo. 208 pp. Price 10 As. net, Post-free.

By Nehemiah Nîlakantha Sâstri Goreh. Translated from the original Hindi, printed and manuscript, by Fitz-Edward Hall, D.C.L., *Oxon.*, H. M.'s. Inspector of Public Instruction for the Central Provinces.

HISTORY OF THE HINDU TRIAD. (Brahma, Vishnu, and Siva) 8vo. 64 pp. 2 As. Post-free, 2½ As.

An account is first given of the earliest gods of the Hindus; the changes which afterwards took place are described; with the development of the Triad as given in the Hindu sacred books.

POPULAR HINDUISM. 8vo. 96 pp. 2½ As. Post-free, 3½ As.

Review of the Hinduism, of the Epic Poems and Puranas, &c.; Rites and Observances; Effects of Hinduism, and Suggested Reforms.

PHILOSOPHIC HINDUISM. 8vo. 72 pp. 2½ As. Post-free, 3 As.

The Upanishads; the Six Schools of Hindu Philosophy; the Minor Schools; Doctrines of Philosophic Hinduism; the Bhagavad Gita; Causes of the Failure of Hindu Philosophy.

THE BRAHMA SAMAJ, AND OTHER MODERN ECLECTIC RELIGIOUS SYSTEMS. 108 pp. 3 As. Post-free, 4 As.

Modern Hindu Theism; Rammohun Roy; Debendranath Tagore; Keshub Chunder Sen; the Sadharan Brahmo Samaj; Madras Brahmoism; Prarthana Samajes.

INDIA HINDU, AND INDIA CHRISTIAN; OR, WHAT HINDUISM HAS DONE FOR INDIA, AND WHAT CHRISTIANITY WOULD DO FOR IT. 8vo. 72 pp. 2½ As. Post-free, 3 As.

Address to thoughtful Hindus, showing how much their country would benefit from the religion which many of them now oppose.

KRISHNA AS DESCRIBED IN THE PURANAS AND BHAGAVAD GITA. 8vo. 72 pp. 2½ As. Post-free, 3 As.

A full account is given of the Krishna Avatara, chiefly taken from the Vishnu Purana, with some extracts from the Bhagavata Purana and the Mahábhárata; the circumstances which led to the great war between the Pandus and Kurus are described; and some of the doctrines of the Bhagavad Gita are examined in detail.

ACCOUNT OF THE TEMPLE OF JAGANNATH AT PURI. 8vo. 48 pp. 1½ As.

The account is taken chiefly from Dr. Rajendralala Mitra's *Antiquities of Orissa*; Hunter's *Gazetteer of India*, Sterling's *Orissa*, &c. With views of the temple, procession, and images.

CHRISTIANITY EXPLAINED TO A HINDU; OR, THE DOCTRINES OF CHRISTIANITY AND HINDUISM COMPARED. 60 pp. 2 As.

Doctrines about God, Creation, the Soul, Karma, Transmigration, Sin, Incarnations, Salvation, Prospects at death, and Comparative Effects.

SWAMI VIVEKANANDA ON HINDUISM. 8vo. 96 pp. 3 As. Post-free, 4 As.

The Swami's Chicago Address is quoted in full and examined; important facts are brought out which he omitted to state.

SWAMI VIVEKANANDA AND HIS GURU. 8vo. 125 pp. 3 As. Post-free, 4 As.

A history of the Swami and his Guru is given; the Swami's boasted success in the West is shown to be untrue by the letters of 45 prominent Americans; the Vedánta philosophy is examined; portraits are given of Schopenhauer and Max Müller, with an estimate of the importance to be attached to their approval of Vedántism.

THE HISTORY OF CHRISTIANITY IN INDIA; WITH ITS PROSPECTS. 8vo. 150 pp. 5 As. Post-free, 6 As.

An account of the early Christian Missions, and the progress of Christianity among the principal nations; with 35 illustrations, including portraits of some eminent Missionaries.

TESTIMONIES OF GREAT MEN TO THE BIBLE AND CHRISTIANITY. 8vo. 45 pp. 1½ As. Post-free, 2 As.

Opinions expressed by great writers, philosophers, scientists, lawyers and statesmen, showing that the Bible and Christianity are firmly believed by the most eminent men of the time.

HOW THE PEOPLE OF ANCIENT EUROPE BECAME CHRISTIANS, AND THE FUTURE RELIGION OF INDIA. 8vo. 48 pp. 1½ As. Post-free, 2 As.

An account of the Eastern and Western Aryans; their common origin; resemblances in language and religion; how Christianity was first brought to Europe; the opposition it encountered, and its final success, with the evidence that it will follow a similar course in India.

CIVILIZATION, ANCIENT AND MODERN, COMPARED; WITH REMARKS ON THE STUDY OF SANSKRIT. 8vo. 48 pp. 1½ As. Post-free, 2 As.

DEVIL-DANCERS, WITCH-FINDERS, RAIN-MAKERS, AND MEDICINE MEN. 4to. 60 pp. 2½ As. Post-free, 3 As.

A full account of these curious and degrading superstitions, prevalent among backward nations in different parts of the world; with 36 illustrations.

TRANSMIGRATION. 12mo. 19 pp. By Rev. Dr. W. Hooper, 1 Anna.

DODDRIDGE'S RISE AND PROGRESS OF RELIGION IN THE SOUL. 12mo. 180 pp. 3 As. Post-free, 4 As.

This is an abridged edition of one of the most useful works on Christianity in the English language.

BARROWS LECTURES. 8vo. 188 pp. 6 As.

Seven Lectures, by the Rev. Dr. J. H. Barrows, on CHRISTIANITY, THE WORLD-WIDE RELIGION.

Pice Papers on Indian Reform, ¼ Anna each.

Some are original; others are abridged from the foregoing for popular use.

1. CAUSES OF INDIAN POVERTY.
2. INDIAN MARRIAGE CUSTOMS.
3. SUPPOSED AND REAL CAUSES OF DISEASE.
4. PATRIOTISM: FALSE AND TRUE.
5. MANAGEMENT OF INFANTS.

6. Debt, and How to Get out of it.
7. The Purdah; or the Seclusion of Indian Women.
8. Caste: its Origin and Effects.
9. Astrology.
10. What has the British Government done for India?
11. Who wrote the Vedas?
12. Manava-Dharma Sastra.
13. The Bhagavad Gita.
14. The Science of the Hindu Sastras.
15. Fevers: their Causes, Treatment and Prevention.
16. Cholera and Bowel Complaints.
17. Animal Worship.
18. Early Marriage; its Evils and Suggested Reforms.
19. Duty to a Wife.
20. The Fruits of Hinduism.
21. Indian Widows, and what should be Done for them.
22. The Advantages of Female Education.
23. Hindu and Christian Worship Compared.
24. Hindu Pilgrimages.
25. Charity: False and True.
26. The Two Watchwords—Custom and Progress.
27. The Value of Pure Water.
28. Charms, Mantras, and other Superstitions.
29. Nautches.
30. Importance of Cleanliness.
31. How to have Healthy Children.
32. Causes of Indian Poverty.
33. Indian Marriage Customs.
34. Eclipses.
35. Family Prayer.
36. Giving Abuse.
37. Shraddhas.
38. Karma or Fate.
39. The Fatherhood of God.
40. The Brotherhood of Man.
41. Hindu and Christian Ideals on Piety.
42. Prayaschitta.

Complete in a volume, half bound, gilt title, 1 Re. Postage, 2 As.

43. An Appeal to Young India.

Papers for Thoughtful Hindus.

No. 1. The Relation between Christianity and Hinduism. 8vo. 32 pp. By the Rev. Dr. Krishna Mohun Banerjea, late Sanskrit Examiner to the Calcutta University. ½ Anna.

The remarkable resemblances, in some respects, between ancient Hinduism and Christianity are pointed out.

No. 2. THE SUPPOSED AND REAL DOCTRINES OF HINDUISM, AS HELD BY EDUCATED HINDUS. 8vo. 32 pp. By the Rev. Nehemiah (Nilakanth) Goreh. ½ Anna.

It is shown that the belief of educated Hindus with regard to God, His Attributes Creation, &c., are not found in the Vedas; but have been derived from Christianity.

No. 3. MORAL COURAGE. 8vo. 32 pp. ½ Anna.

A lecture by the Bishop of Bombay.

No. 4. THE IMPORTANCE OF RELIGION. 8vo. 48 pp. ¾ Anna.

An appeal to the young, by John Foster, author of Essays on *Decision of Character*.

No. 5. CHRISTIANITY, OR—WHAT? 8vo. 16 pp. ¼ Anna. By the Rev. H. Rice.

Christianity is shown to be the only religion which meets the wants of man.

No. 6. THE SENSE OF SIN IN THE LIGHT OF HISTORY. A Lecture by the Rev. F. W. KELLETT, M.A., Madras Christian College. 8vo. 20 pp. ½ Anna.

It is shown that the deeper the sense of sin, the more mature the religious life.

No. 7. BISHOP CALDWELL ON KRISHNA AND THE BHAGAVAD GITA. 8vo. 32 pp. ¾ Anna.

A reprint of Remarks on the late Hon. Sadagopah Charloo's introduction to a Reprint of a Pamphlet entitled, "*Theosophy of the Hindus;*" with a preface by the Rev. J. L. Wyatt.

No. 8. THE DUTIES OF EDUCATED YOUNG MEN TO THEIR COUNTRY. 8vo. 16 pp. ½ Anna.

An address, by the Rev. H. Ballantine, at a Meeting of the Ahmednagar Debating Society. Translated from the Marathi.

No. 9. CHRIST THE FULFILMENT OF HINDUISM. 8vo. 23 pp. ½ Anna.

A lecture by the Rev. F. W. KELLETT, M.A., Madras Christian College.

No. 10. VEDANTISM. 8vo. 21 pp. ½ Anna.

By the Rev. Lal Behari Day, with numerous Sanskrit quotations.

No. 11. THE DEFECTIVENESS OF BRAHMOISM. 8vo. 24 pp. ½ Anna.

A Lecture by the Rev. Lal Behari Day.

No. 12. PRELIMINARY DIALOGUES ON IMPORTANT QUESTIONS IN INDIA. 8vo. 74 pp 2 As. Post-free, 2½ As.

By a member of the Oxford Mission, Calcutta. Hindu and Christian Conceptions of God, Theism *versus* Pantheism, Personality, Merit and Demerit, Sin, &c.

No. 13. HELPS TO TRUTH-SEEKERS. 8vo. 32 pp. 1 Anna.

By the Rev. H. Rice. Current objections to Christianity considered.

No. 14. HINDU PANTHEISM. 8vo. 18 pp. ½ Anna.

From *Anti-theistic Theories*, by Professor Flint, an able writer.

Progress.

This is a monthly illustrated Periodical for the educated classes in India and Ceylon. The subscription is only 8 As. a year, with postage 14 As. Three copies may be sent for ½ anna postage.

The Periodical is specially recommended to TEACHERS. It would give new ideas to their pupils, while the page for students would be very useful to those preparing for examinations.

Orders to be addressed to Mr. A. T. SCOTT, Tract Depôt, MADRAS.

S. P. C. K. PRESS, VEPERY, MADRAS—1897.